This book belongs to:

....

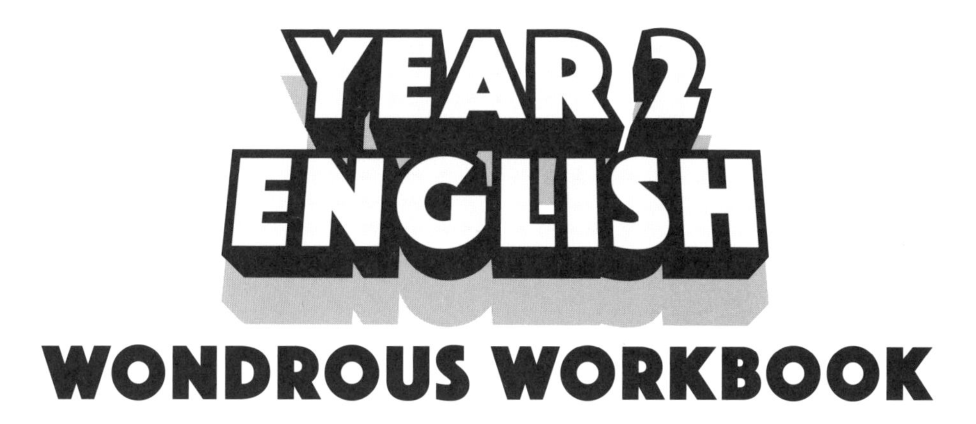

mrswordsmith.com

Brick

Plato

Yin & Yang

Grit

Armie

MEET THE CHARACTERS

CONTENTS

Welcome to the Year 2 Wondrous Workbook!

What's inside?

In this book, you will find everything you need to soar through English in Year 2. It is divided into six chapters: **Grammar**, **Punctuation**, **Vocabulary**, **Spelling**, **Reading and Writing** and **Handwriting**. Each chapter combines targeted teaching of key skills, illustrations and activities. It's perfect for those learning something for the first time and for those who are just revising!

How do I use it?

However you want to! Start in the middle, start at the end or you could even start at the beginning if you're feeling traditional. Take it slowly and do one section at a time, or charge through the pages like a gorilla on the loose! Don't worry if something is too difficult. You'll get there in the end and there are tips and reminders to help you along the way.

Look out for this icon at the beginning of a new topic. It tells you that there's some important learning to do before you start answering the questions!

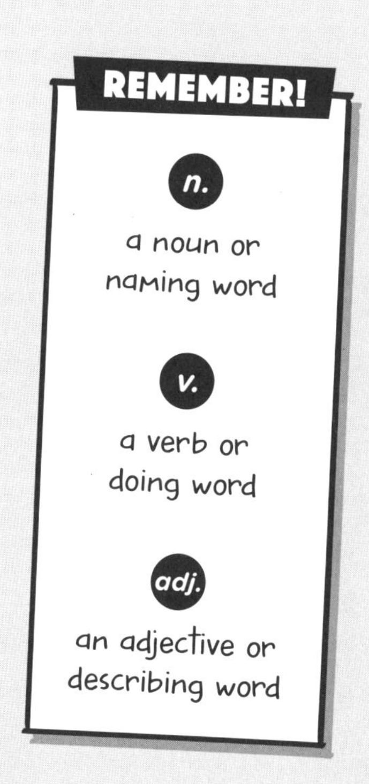

How do I check my answers?

There's an answer key at the back! Checking answers is an important part of learning. Take care to notice and remember the ones you didn't know.

Oh, and please excuse Mrs Wordsmith's cast of out-of-control animals. They pop up all over the place and are usually up to no good.

Now, go and have some fun! And who knows, you might learn something along the way.

GRAMMAR

Grammar teaches you how to use different kinds of words (like verbs, nouns or adjectives) and to form sentences in the past, present or future tense. When you master some basic grammar rules, you have the power to talk or write about anything.

Verbs are doing and being words.

A **doing word** describes an action. For example, '**jump**' is a doing word.

A **being word** describes a state of being. For example, '**am**' is a being word.

Oz **jumps**.

I **am** sorry.

1 Circle the verbs.

giggle **eat** **blue** **horse**

catch **like** **leaf**

2 Underline the verbs in these sentences.

a. Brick runs home.

b. The elephant dances.

c. Bogart swims in puddles.

d. The sun shines brightly.

e. Yin chases Yang.

f. Armie reads every day.

b. Verbs can end in **-ing** to show that something **is happening** (right now) or **was happening** (in the past).

Shang High **is juggling**.

Shang High **was juggling**.

3 Complete these sentences.

These sentences are about something that **is happening** right now. Fill in the blanks with the **verb** that makes the most sense.

playing **eating** **laughing**

a. Bearnice is .... at the funny joke.

b. Bogart is .... a video game.

c. Plato is .... 24 tacos.

4 Complete these sentences.

These sentences are about something that **was happening** in the past. Fill in the blanks with the **verb** that makes the most sense.

kicking **baking** **drinking**

a. Brick was .... a healthy smoothie.

b. Yin was .... the ball.

c. Plato was .... a chocolate fudge cake.

A noun is the **name of a person or animal**, **place** or **thing**.

EXAMPLES

Person or animal – for example, "**Yin** loves **fish**."

Place – for example, "She goes to **school** in **Australia**."

Thing – for example, "They spoke on the **phone**."

1 Match the nouns to the pictures.

Draw a line from each picture to a noun.
Is this noun a person or animal, place or thing?
Then, draw a line from the noun to the category it fits in.

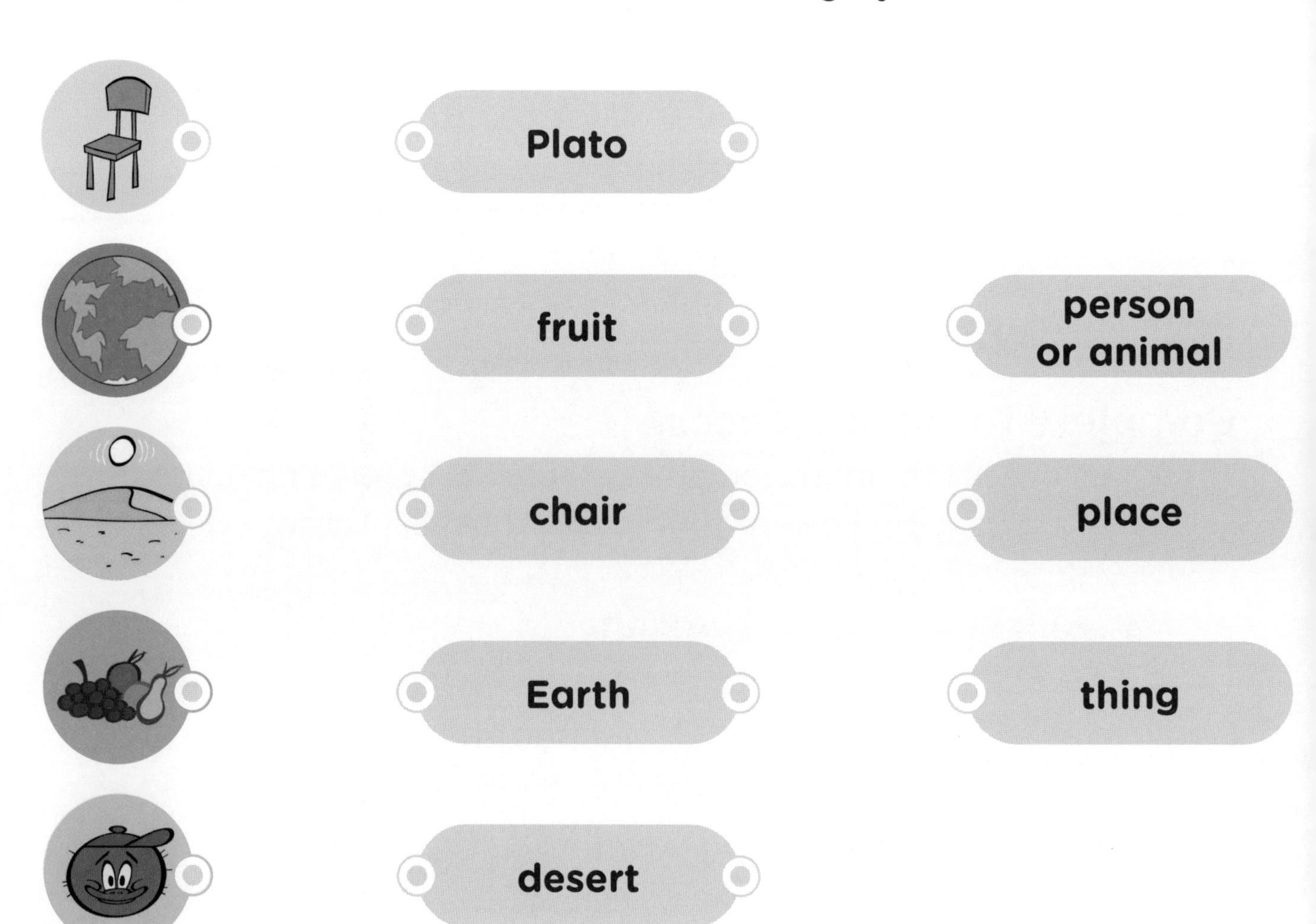

2 Circle the nouns.

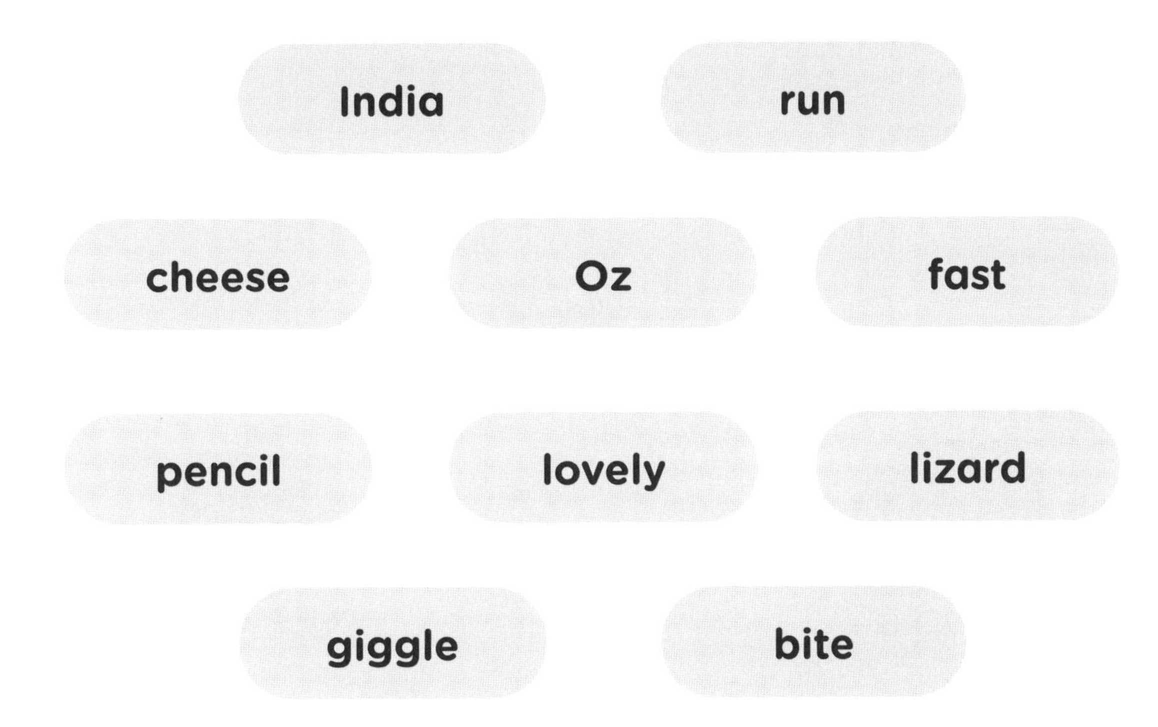

3 Underline the nouns in these sentences.

Read through these sentences and find the nouns.
Remember, some sentences will have more than one noun!

a. The pizza is very tasty.

b. Armie loves the library.

c. The frog jumped up.

d. Plato is travelling to Brazil.

e. Yin and Yang play in the garden.

f. Oz loves pink marshmallows.

Tall is a descriptive word.
A descriptive word is an **adjective**.

Adjectives are words that describe nouns, like a **tall** tree.

EXAMPLES

a **shiny** ring

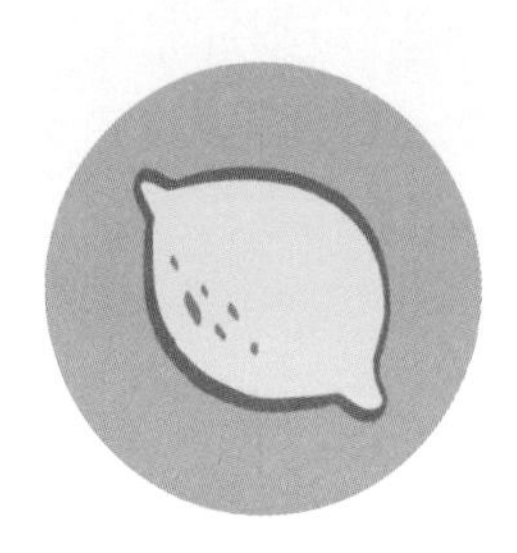

a **sour** lemon

a **warm** pie

1 Underline the adjectives in the phrases below.

a. a huge elephant

b. an evil robot

c. a slimy frog

d. a beautiful sunset

e. a fried egg

f. a prickly hedgehog

g. an unusual laugh

h. a brave lion

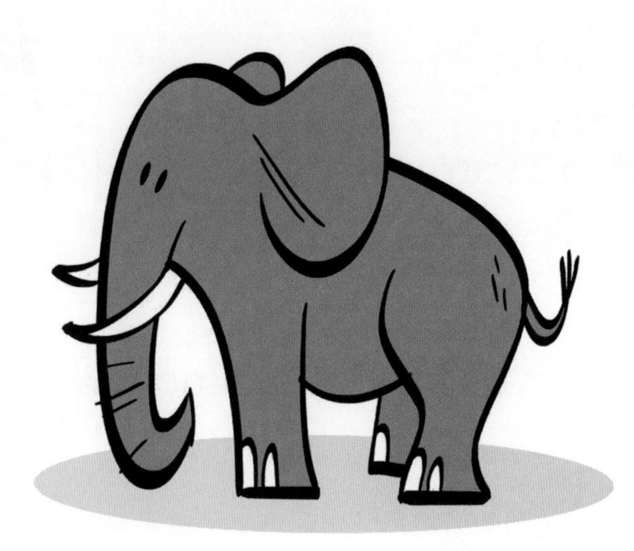

2 Choose the adjective that best describes the noun.

Write it in the gaps.

red	tall	fluffy	hot
howling	cosy	sticky	spicy

a. a hot .... bath

b. the .... giraffe

c. a .... pepper

d. the .... honey

e. the .... kitten

f. a .... apple

g. the .... home

h. a .... wolf

Adverbs describe verbs. Remember, a verb is a doing or being word. Adverbs describe how or when we do things. They often end in **-ly**.

"How did you fix the vase?" "We fixed it **carefully**!"

Adverbs are linked to verbs, but they can go in different places in the sentence.

She screamed **suddenly**. **Suddenly**, she screamed.

We will be focusing on adverbs that come after the verb.

EXAMPLES

He dances **gracefully**.

She ran **quickly**.

The lion roared **loudly**.

1 Circle the adverbs and underline the verbs.

a. They laughed happily.

b. The snail moves slowly.

c. They ate greedily.

d. He sighed sadly.

e. She spoke quietly.

f. My tummy rumbled loudly.

2 Complete these sentences.

Use the list of adverbs below to fill in the gaps.
Read the sentences aloud to help you.

slowly **tearfully** **joyfully** **messily**

a. Brick walked .... through the desert.

b. Plato ate his food ....

c. Armie watched the film ....

d. Plato skipped ....

Plural nouns show that there are more than one of that noun.
There are different spelling rules to help us show this.

To turn most nouns into plural nouns, just add -**s**.

Add -**es** when the noun ends in -**s**, -**ch**, -**sh**, -**x** or -**z**.

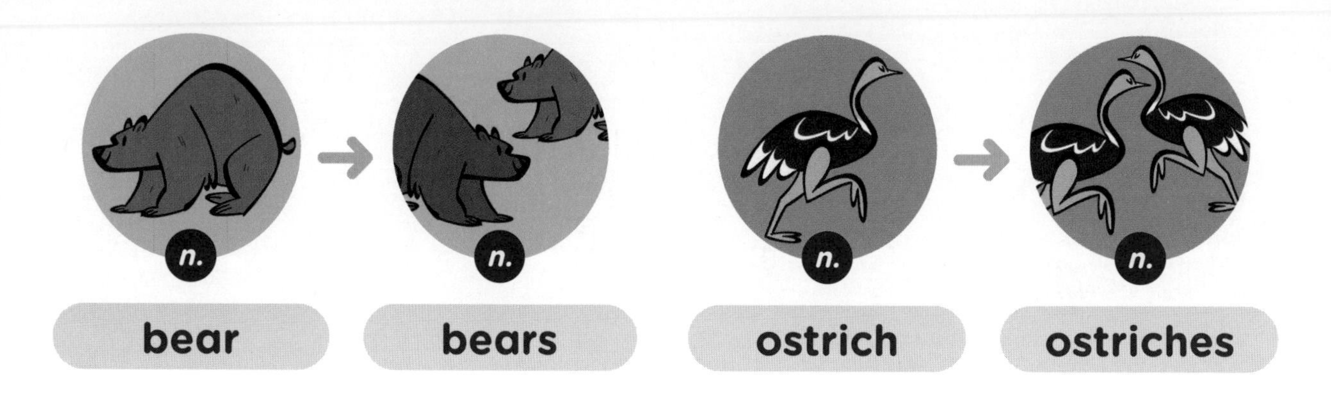

1 Turn these nouns into plural nouns!

Write -**s** or -**es** to complete each word.

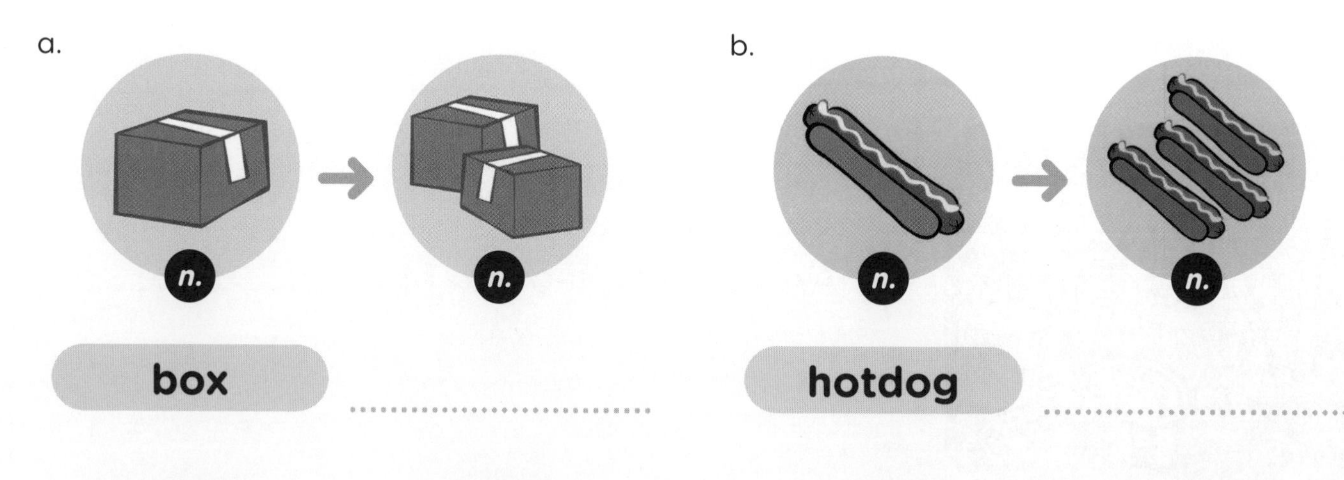

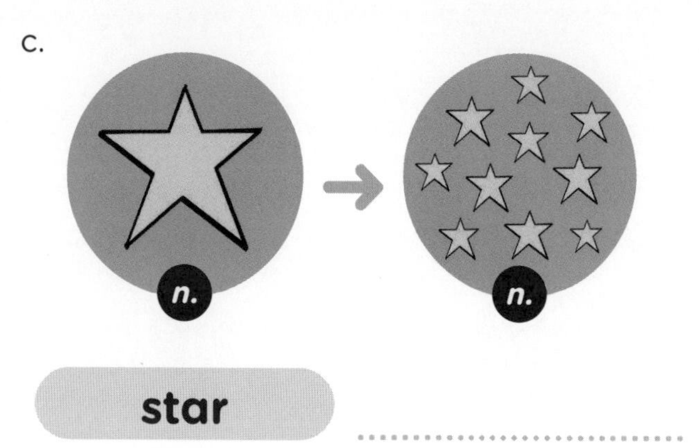

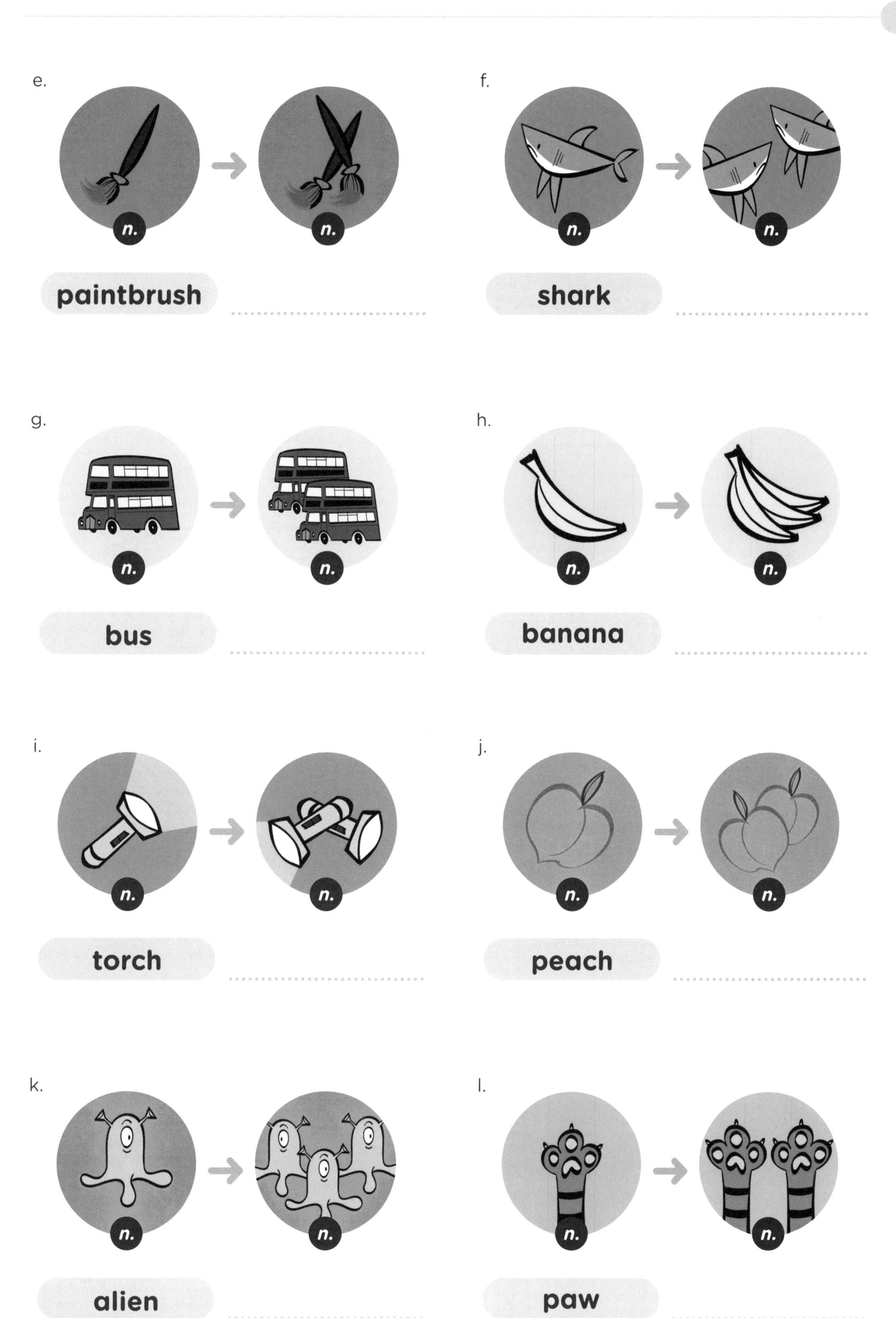
e.
n.
n.
paintbrush
f.
n.
n.
shark
g.
n.
n.
bus
h.
n.
n.
banana
i.
n.
n.
torch
j.
n.
n.
peach
k.
n.
n.
alien
l.
n.
n.
paw

If a noun ends in a **vowel** + **-y**, just add **-s**.

monkey → monkeys

2 Can you change these nouns into plurals?

a. day → ....

b. boy → ....

c. key → ....

d. tray → ....

e. toy → ....

If a noun ends in a **consonant** + **-y**, then remove the **-y** and add **-ies**.

puppy → puppies

3 Can you change these nouns into plurals?

a. fly → ....

b. penny → ....

c. city → ....

d. fairy → ....

e. baby → ....

4 Write the correct spelling to finish each sentence.

Remember what we have just learned.

Rule 1. Add -**s** to most nouns.
Rule 2. Add -**es** when the noun ends in -**s**, -**ch**, -**sh**, -**x** or -**z**.
Rule 3. If a noun ends in a **vowel** + -**y**, just add -**s**.
Rule 4. If a noun ends in a **consonant** + -**y**, then remove the -**y** and add -**ies**.

a. Did you see two ~~fox~~ ....foxes.... in the garden last night?

b. Shang High went to three birthday ~~party~~ ....!

c. Sometimes, the best gifts come in the smallest ~~box~~ ....

d. Brick asked the genie for a hundred new ~~toy~~ ....

e. Armie is running out of space for all of his ~~book~~ ....!

f. Grit counted six yellow ~~lorry~~ .... and four red ones.

g. Oz visited three ~~beach~~ .... today.

h. Armie wrote a story about two friendly ~~witch~~ ....

i. Plato ate a record-breaking

number of ~~pie~~ ....

An expanded noun phrase is a group of words that tell you about a noun. Remember, a noun is a person or animal, place or thing, like a **tree**.

EXAMPLES

These are examples of expanded noun phrases that give more information about the noun **tree**.

The tall **tree**.

The tall, leafy **tree**.

The **tree** with green leaves.

The **tree** that grows apples.

We are going to practise making expanded noun phrases using an adjective before the noun, like **the tall tree**.

1 Draw a line to connect each adjective to a noun!

Then, draw a line connecting the expanded noun phrase to the matching picture.

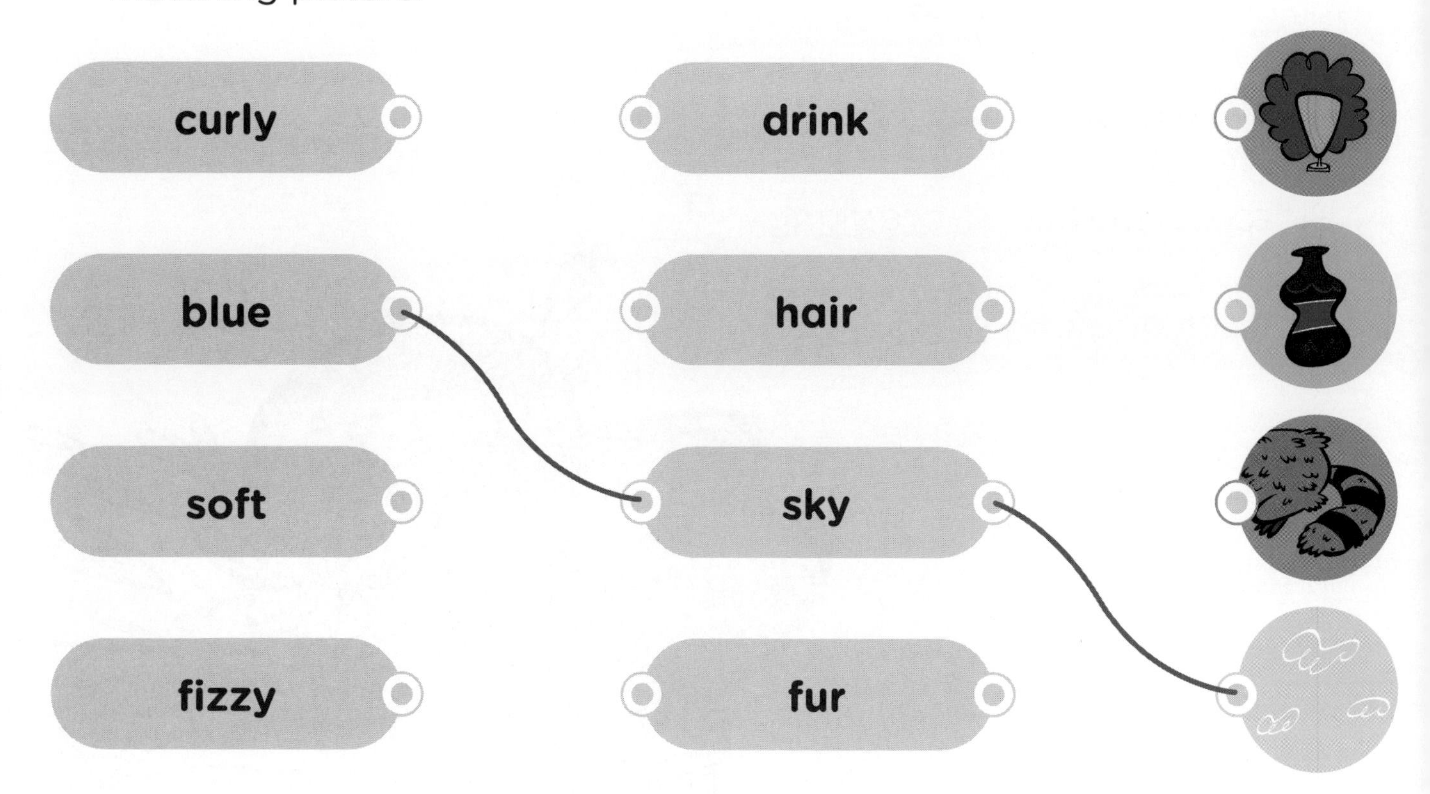

2 Fill in the blanks with adjectives of your own.

Here are some nouns. Can you think of adjectives that will turn them into expanded noun phrases?

a.

the

red

car

b.

the

ring

REMEMBER!

Some adjectives go better with certain nouns than others. For example, a tall tree makes more sense than a blue tree.

c.

the

friend

d.

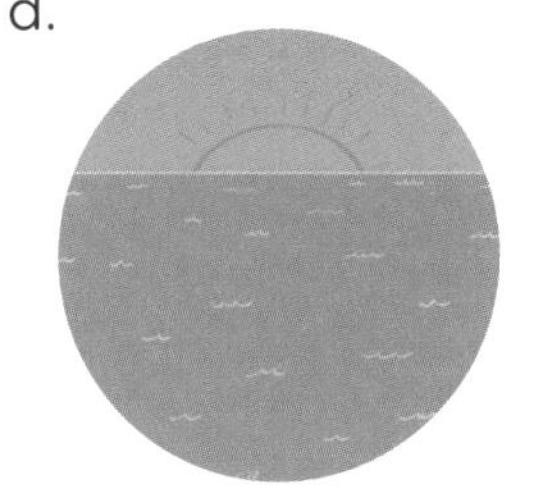

the

sea

e.

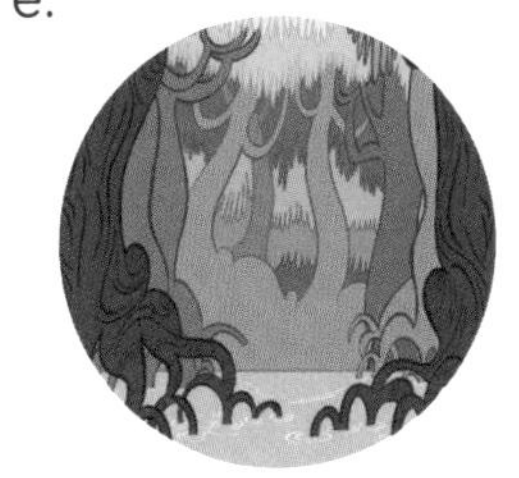

the

jungle

f.

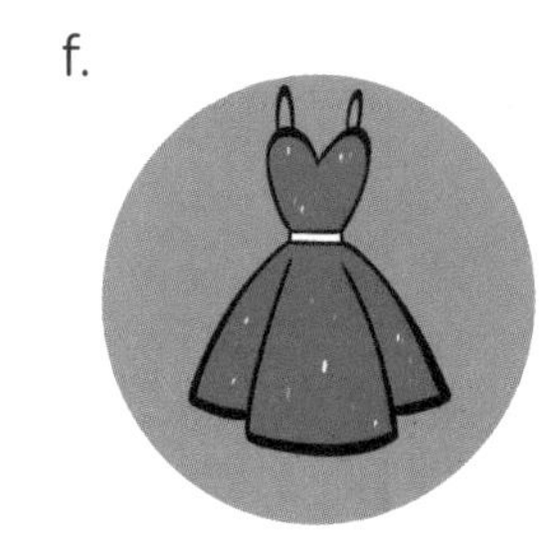

the

dress

g.

the

leaf

h.

the

banana

i.

the

snake

j.

the

pizza

Tense tells us when something takes place. Things can happen in the past, present or future. When a sentence has more than one verb in it, they are usually in the same tense.

EXAMPLES

The verbs in this sentence are in the present tense:

After school, I **walk** to the park and **play** football.

The verbs in this sentence are in the past tense:

Yesterday, I **listened** to music and **talked** to my friends.

REMEMBER!

Regular past tense verbs end in -ed.

1 Help Oz write her diary in the present tense!

Oz is writing about what she does on Saturdays, so she is using the present tense. Underline the correct form of these verbs.

Dear Diary,

a. Every Saturday, I run and **play** **played** in the park.

b. I eat lunch and **watched** **watch** a funny film.

c. I **cuddle** **cuddled** my teddy bear.

2 Help Grit write his diary in the past tense!

Grit is writing about yesterday, so he is using the past tense.
Underline the correct form of these verbs.

Dear Diary,

a. Yesterday, I visited the beach and **play** **played** in the sand.

b. A crab **pinched** **pinch** my toe!

c. It really hurt! I **scream** **screamed** very loudly!

3 Help Bearnice write in the irregular past tense!

Bearnice is writing about the irregular day she had yesterday!
Underline the correct form of these verbs.

Dear Diary,

a. Yesterday, I looked down and **see** **saw** a worm between my toes.

b. I **feel** **felt** sad for the worm because he was all alone.

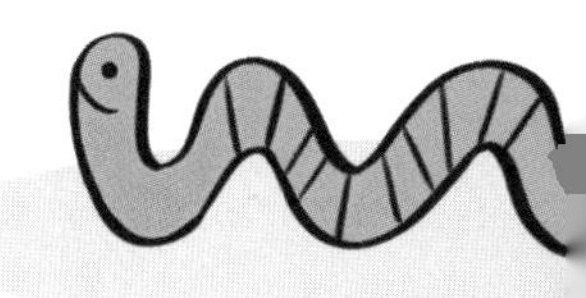

c. So I picked him up and **bring** **brought** him home.

A sentence is a complete idea that makes sense by itself.
There are four different types of complete sentences: statements, questions, commands and exclamation sentences.

A **statement** expresses a fact, idea or opinion. This is the most common type of sentence. It usually ends with a full stop, for example:

It is raining.

1 Circle the statement.

a. When did Brick jump into the water?

b. Brick jumped into the water.

c. Where is Brick?

A **question** asks something that needs an answer.
It ends with a question mark, for example:

When did it start raining?

2 Circle the question.

a. Shang High is very tall.

b. Shang High is hiding.

c. Where is Shang High?

A **command** tells someone to do something.
It can end with a full stop or exclamation mark, for example:

Put up your umbrella.

3 Circle the command.

a. Who is stuck in a tree?

b. Yin and Yang are stuck in a tree.

c. Help me.

An **exclamation** sentence tells something with surprise or strong feeling. It is a full sentence that starts with "what" or "how" and ends with an exclamation mark, for example:

What a tiny umbrella that is!

4 Circle the exclamation sentence.

a. Who is making a sandwich?

b. Oz is making a peanut butter and jam sandwich.

c. What a lot of jam Oz is using!

5 Label the sentence types.

Each image has a statement **S**, question **Q**, command **C** and exclamation sentence **E**. Label each sentence with the right letter.

a. What a strange banana this is!

Plato is confused.

Where did this banana come from?

Don't eat that.

b. Who is hugging Bogart?

Bearnice is hugging Bogart.

How tightly Bearnice is squeezing Bogart!

Let me go, Bearnice.

c. Yin and Yang are not blinking.

Start the stopwatch, Bogart.

What a long staring contest this is!

When will the staring contest end?

d. Where did Brick eat his dinner?

What a mess Brick has made!

Brick is covered in spaghetti.

Clean up this mess.

e. Yang is in the bathroom.

Where is Yang?

Stop that!

What a lot of toilet paper that is!

f. Plato is wearing a hat and a tutu.

Look at Plato.

Why is Plato wearing that hat?

How silly Plato looks!

A and **an** are articles. They appear before nouns or noun phrases.

A loves consonant sounds!
A loves being close to consonant sounds like **t**, **c** and **sh**, for example:

a trumpet, **a c**andle, **a sh**oe

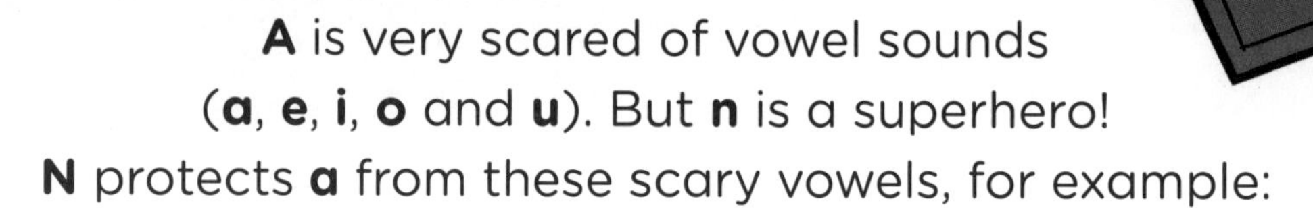

A is very scared of vowel sounds (**a**, **e**, **i**, **o** and **u**). But **n** is a superhero!
N protects **a** from these scary vowels, for example:

an apple, **an e**lephant, **an u**mbrella

1 Draw a line connecting the noun to a or an.

Don't forget to keep **a** safe from those scary vowels!

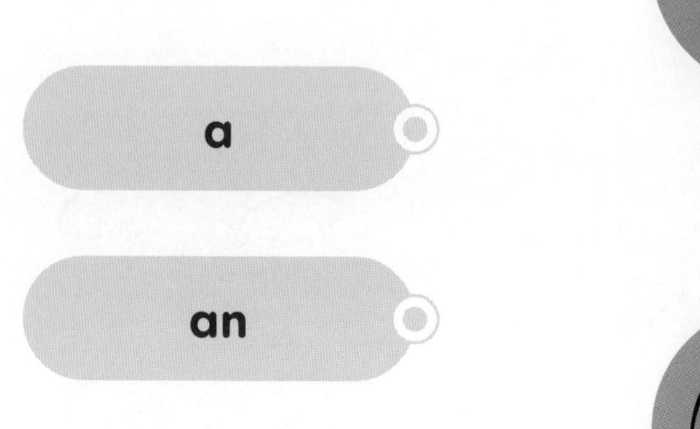

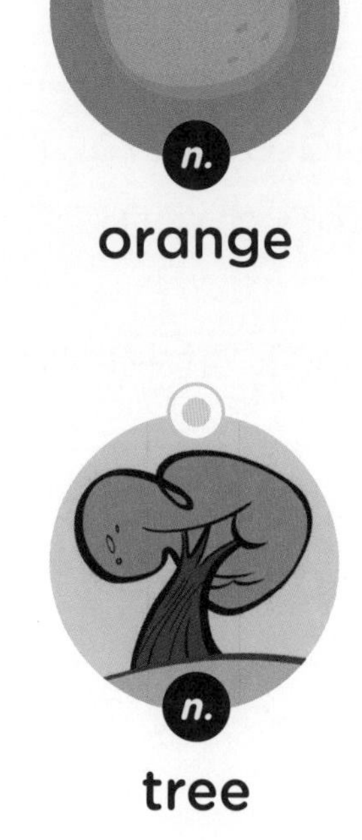

2 Complete these sentences with **a** or **an**.

a. Armie dreamed of being .... astronaut.

b. Shang High took .... cold shower.

c. Grit has .... hole in his trousers!

d. Bogart held up .... umbrella.

e. Plato dreams of owning .... food truck.

Conjunctions are joining words that connect two parts of a sentence, like **and**, **but** and **or**. These words are very useful when you are writing.

EXAMPLES

I walked to school **and** I walked home.

I ate my lunch **but** I'm still hungry.

I will call you **or** send you a text.

1 Join these sentences together.

Draw a line from the first part of each sentence to the second part.

Brick grabbed his bicycle **and**	Bearnice's snoring kept her awake.
Grit didn't mean to be rude **but**	he was making music.
Oz was very tired **but**	cycled straight to the aquarium.
Shang High was usually listening to music **or**	a piece of cake.
At three o'clock, Plato had a cup of tea **and**	he just wasn't in the mood for talking.

2 Complete these sentences.

Fill in the blanks using the best conjunction for each sentence.

and	or	but

a. Yin wondered if Oz would prefer to have a picnic .... go to the cinema.

b. Grit really wanted a hotdog .... he wasn't sure if he had enough money.

c. There was something strange going on .... Armie wanted to get to the bottom of it.

d. Bearnice had a crayon .... she didn't have any paper.

e. Plato zipped up his raincoat .... headed out into the storm.

Here are some more useful conjunctions to use in your writing! These allow you to extend sentences and give more information.

EXAMPLES

The car stopped **when** the light turned red.

I am very excited **because** it's my birthday!

You can have a cupcake **if** you give me a cookie.

Did you know **that** pandas spend twelve hours eating every day?

3 Join these sentences together.

Draw a line from the first part of each sentence to the second part.

I can't wait to have a birthday party **when**	I was starving.
I ate ten waffles for breakfast **because**	crocodiles can't stick their tongues out!
I don't want to get soaked **if**	I turn seven!
I didn't know **that**	it starts raining.

4 Complete these sentences.

Fill in the blanks using the best conjunction for each sentence.

because **if** **when** **that**

a. Bearnice enjoyed funny films .... she loved to laugh.

b. Brick screamed .... the spider landed on his forehead.

c. Armie didn't dance .... he was too shy.

d. Yang wondered .... she would ever get to travel into space.

e. Armie could not believe .... he was unable to lick his elbow!

f. Oz knew that she could do anything .... she put her mind to it.

5 Can you help Armie with his writing?

Armie has started these sentences but can't finish them. Use the **conjunctions** to work out what should come next.

a. I woke up very early this morning **because...**

....

....

....

....

....

....

....

b. I felt scared **when...**

....

....

....

....

....

....

....

c. I couldn't stop laughing **because...**

d. I kicked the ball as hard as I could **and...**

You have already learned that adverbs describe verbs. Remember, a verb is a doing or being word. Adverbs describe how or when we do things. They often end in -**ly**.

For example, luckily is an **adverb**.

Luckily, there is more to learn!

Adverbials are **words or phrases** (more than one word) that do the same job as adverbs.

EXAMPLES

Adverbials can describe **how**, **when** or **where** a verb happens. We will be focusing on when.

Bearnice is going swimming in an hour.

This adverbial tells us when the action of the verb will happen.

Adverbials can show **how quickly** or **slowly** something happens.

Bogart vanished in a flash.

This adverbial tells us that Bogart vanished very quickly.

1 Find the adverbials in these sentences.

Underline the words that tell you when, how quickly or how slowly the verb happened.

a. Grit ate toast in the morning.

b. The alien disappeared in the blink of an eye.

c. Bearnice forgot to brush her teeth last night.

d. Brick ran as quick as lightning.

e. All of a sudden, everything went dark!

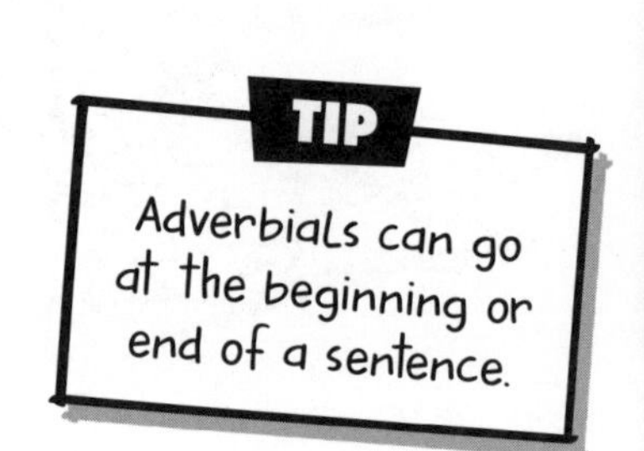

2 Complete these sentences by adding the adverbial.

Some adverbials might work in more than one sentence.

bit by bit	after a short while	later today	in no time at all

a. Everything was back to normal ....

b. Yang finished her homework ....

c. Grit has football practice ....

d. They moved into their new home ....

3 Complete these sentences by adding the adverbial.

Some adverbials might work in more than one sentence.

Moments later	Suddenly	Eventually	Yesterday

a. ...., the painting was stolen.

b. ...., Grit arrived back home.

c. ...., Oz lost her favourite teddy bear.

d. ...., the door swung open.

PUNCTUATION

When we talk, we use the tone of our voices to make our meaning clear. When we write, we rely on punctuation instead. In this chapter, you'll practise four key punctuation skills.

You need to remember to use capital letters:

At the **start** of each sentence

When writing **names of people**, **places**, **the days of the week** and **months**

When writing **I**

FOR EXAMPLE:

Yesterday, **G**rit and **I** went shopping.

On **T**uesday, **O**z is going on holiday to **C**hina.

1 What's wrong with these sentences?

Circle the letters that should be capitalised.

a. yin and yang love to braid bearnice's hair.

b. every tuesday, armie writes in his diary for half an hour.

c. tomorrow, plato and i will have a food fight.

d. it's dinner time and yin is very hungry.

e. yesterday, plato ran out of toilet paper!

f. after a long day at school, oz fell asleep on the swings.

2 Rewrite these sentences in the correct order.

Use the capital letters as clues.
Don't forget to add a full stop at the end.

a. cake eats He

....

....

b. is cold Ice

....

....

c. are green Trees

....

....

d. love I December

....

....

3 Rewrite these sentences in the correct order.

Don't forget to add capital letters and a full stop at the end.

a. walked they home

....

....

b. fridays on she swims

....

....

Commas help the reader. They can be used to separate items in a list.

You need a comma between all the items, except the last two. Put **and** or **or** between the last two.

FOR EXAMPLE:

Oz is friends with Yin, Yang, Bearnice, Grit and Shang High.

Bogart wants cheese, cake, pizza or ice cream for dinner.

1 Fix these sentences.

Add commas in the correct places.

a. Bearnice went to the shop to buy apples bananas cookies eggs and cheese.

b. Yang could play with Brick Bogart or Armie.

c. Plato likes to swim in pools lakes streams and rivers.

d. Oz could sit on the bed chair toilet or sofa.

e. Grit visited a farm with lots of chickens pigs cows ducks and mice.

f. Yin's pencil case contains pencils pens and rulers.

2 Time for a trip to the ice cream parlour!

Each cone can fit five flavoured scoops. Complete the sentences to order five scoops. Don't forget to use commas in your list.

a. Can I please have ....

....?

b. Can Bogart please have ....

....?

c. Can Plato please have ....

....?

Apostrophes have several functions.

Sometimes, apostrophes can show **belonging**.

You can show that something belongs to someone (or something) by using an **apostrophe** and an **s**.

FOR EXAMPLE:

Shang High's jumper

This means the jumper belongs to Shang High.

Grit's race track

This means the race track belongs to Grit.

1 Circle the apostrophes in each of these phrases.

a. Yang's scarf

b. Plato's tacos

c. Bogart's ice cream

d. Brick's family

2 Add an apostrophe to each of these phrases.

a. Yins teddy bear

b. Grits skateboard

c. Bricks new trainers

d. Bogarts telescope

e. Armies book

f. Platos frying pan

3 Rewrite these sentences.

Use an apostrophe to show belonging.

a. This phone belongs to Grit.

....

....

b. This robot belongs to Bogart.

....

....

c. This hat belongs to Bearnice.

....

....

d. This laptop belongs to Armie.

....

....

e. This cake belongs to Plato.

....

....

f. This ring belongs to Yin.

....

....

Apostrophes have several functions.

Sometimes, apostrophes can show where letters are missing in shortened versions of words.

These shortened versions of words are called **contractions**.

FOR EXAMPLE:

I am late for school! → **I'm** late for school!

She is on her bike! → **She's** on her bike!

1 Circle the correct contraction.

Read these phrases. Check which letters are crossed out and circle the correct contraction on the right.

TIP!

Remember, the apostrophe replaces the missing letter or letters.

I am → I ~~a~~m a. **I'm** **I'am**

You are → You ~~a~~re b. **Your'e** **You're**

She is → She ~~i~~s c. **She's** **Sh'es**

We are → We ~~are~~ d. **We're** **Wer'e**

They are → They ~~are~~ e. **Th'eyre** **They're**

You will → You ~~wi~~ll f. **Yo'ull** **You'll**

Was not → Was n~~o~~t g. **Wa'snt** **Wasn't**

Did not → Did n~~o~~t h. **Didn't** **Did'nt**

Do not → Do n~~o~~t i. **D'ont** **Don't**

2 Rewrite these sentences.

Use an apostrophe to show where letters are missing.

a. We are flying.

d. You will fix it!

b. I am sorry.

e. She is very tired.

c. It was not me.

f. Do not hurt my teddy bear!

VOCABULARY

Vocabulary is probably the most important part of learning to read and write. You wouldn't be able to read this sentence if you didn't know what all the words meant! Knowing lots of synonyms helps you express yourself more accurately. Learning about prefixes and suffixes gives you clues about what new words mean when you come across them.

Prefixes are groups of letters that are added to the beginning of words to change their meaning.

Adding the prefix **un-** means **not**:
un + kind = **unkind**, meaning **not kind**

Adding the prefix **re-** means **again**:
re + write = **rewrite**, meaning **to write again**

1 Transform these stories with the right prefixes!

Pick the correct prefix and write the whole word in the gap to complete the sentence. Say it out loud to make sure it makes sense.

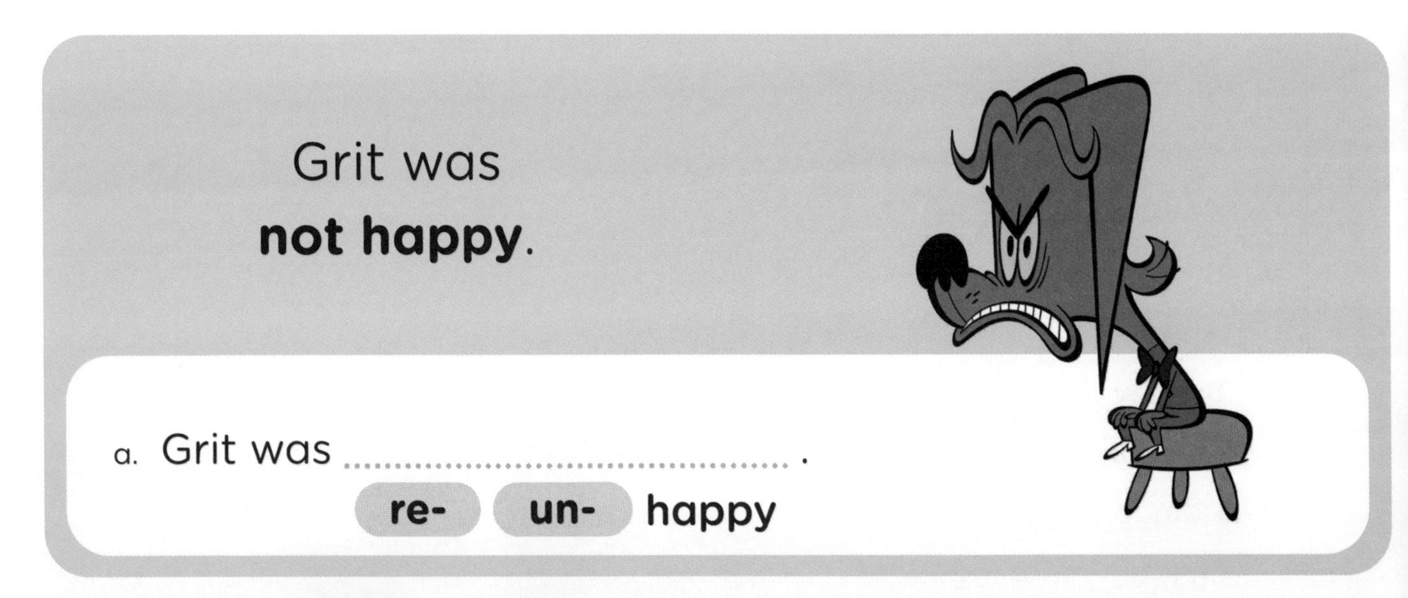

Grit was **not happy**.

a. Grit was ....

re- **un-** **happy**

Plato had to **do** his homework **again**.

b. Plato had to .... his homework.

re- **un-** **do**

Brick did **not zip** up his bag.

c. Brick's bag is ....

re- **un-** zipped

Oz's collection of shoes was **not tidy**.

d. Oz's collection of shoes was ....

re- **un-** tidy

The game was so fun that Armie decided to **play** it **again**.

e. Armie decided to .... the game.

re- **un-** play

Suffixes are groups of letters that are added to the end of words to change their meaning.

Adding the suffix **-ful** means **with**:
care + ful = **careful**, meaning **with care**

Adding the suffix **-less** means **without**:
hope + less = **hopeless**, meaning **without hope**

1 Transform these stories with the right suffixes!

Pick the correct suffix and write the whole word in the gap to complete the sentence. Say it out loud to make sure it makes sense.

Plato's painting was **full of colour**.

a. Plato's painting was ....

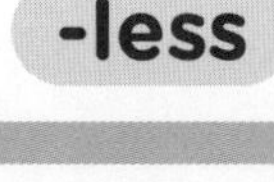

colour **-ful** **-less**

Without fear, the knight battled the dragon.

b. The .... knight battled the dragon.

fear **-ful** **-less**

The experiment was **a great success**!

c. The experiment was .... !

success **-ful** **-less**

The wait seemed **like it would never end**.

d. The wait seemed ....

end **-ful** **-less**

Plato put **a lot of thought** into his apology.

e. Plato gave a .... apology.

thought **-ful** **-less**

Suffixes are groups of letters that are added to the end of words to change their meaning.

You can add the suffix **-ment** to turn some verbs into nouns:
pay + ment = **payment**

You can add the suffix **-ness** to turn some adjectives into nouns:
quiet + ness = **quietness**

1 Transform these stories with the right suffixes!

Pick the correct suffix and write the whole word in the gap to complete the sentence. Say it out loud to make sure it makes sense.

Yin and Yang **agreed** to build the best snowman ever.

a. Yin and Yang were in ....

agree **-ment** **-ness**

Shang High was **very kind** to Plato.

b. Shang High showed Plato ....

kind **-ment** **-ness**

Plato was **very sad**.

c. Plato felt a lot of ....

sad **-ment** **-ness**

Grit was **very entertained** by what he saw on the TV.

d. The TV was Grit's favourite kind of ....

entertain **-ment** **-ness**

Bearnice, Shang High and Grit were afraid of the **dark**.

e. The .... made them afraid.

dark **-ment** **-ness**

Compound words are made of two words that are joined together to make one word, like **doorbell**.

door + bell = **doorbell**

1 Fill in the blanks to create the compound words!

Use the pictures to help you.

a.

b.................. + b.................. = ...

b.

c.................. + g.................. = ...

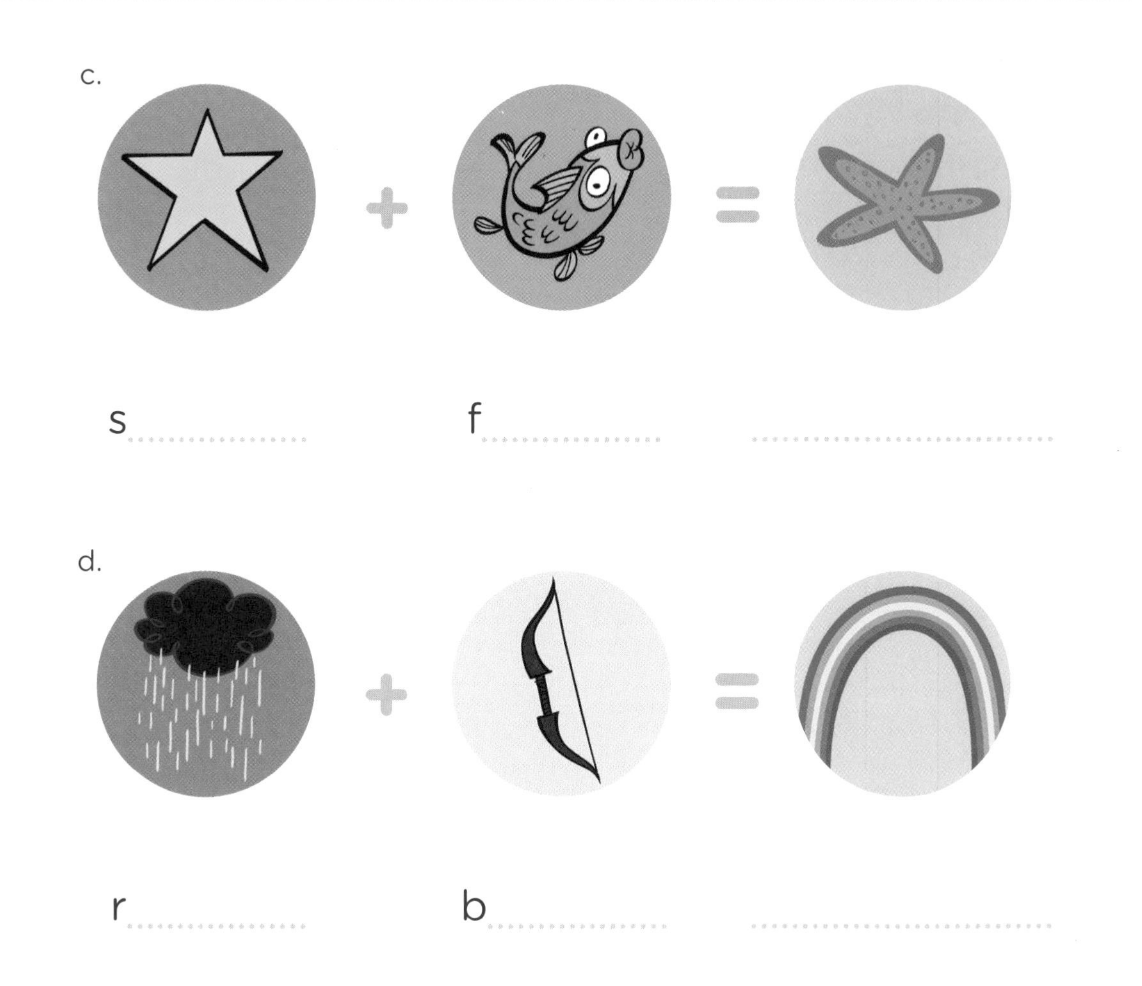

c.

s ……… + f ……… = ………

d.

r ……… + b ……… = ………

2 Can you work out what the missing words are?

These compound words have been replaced by pictures.
Can you fill in the blanks?

a. ……… + fly =

b. news + ……… =

c. ……… + fish =

3 Match the right words to make compound words.

Draw a line from a word in the first column to a word in the second column. Then, draw a line connecting those words to a picture.

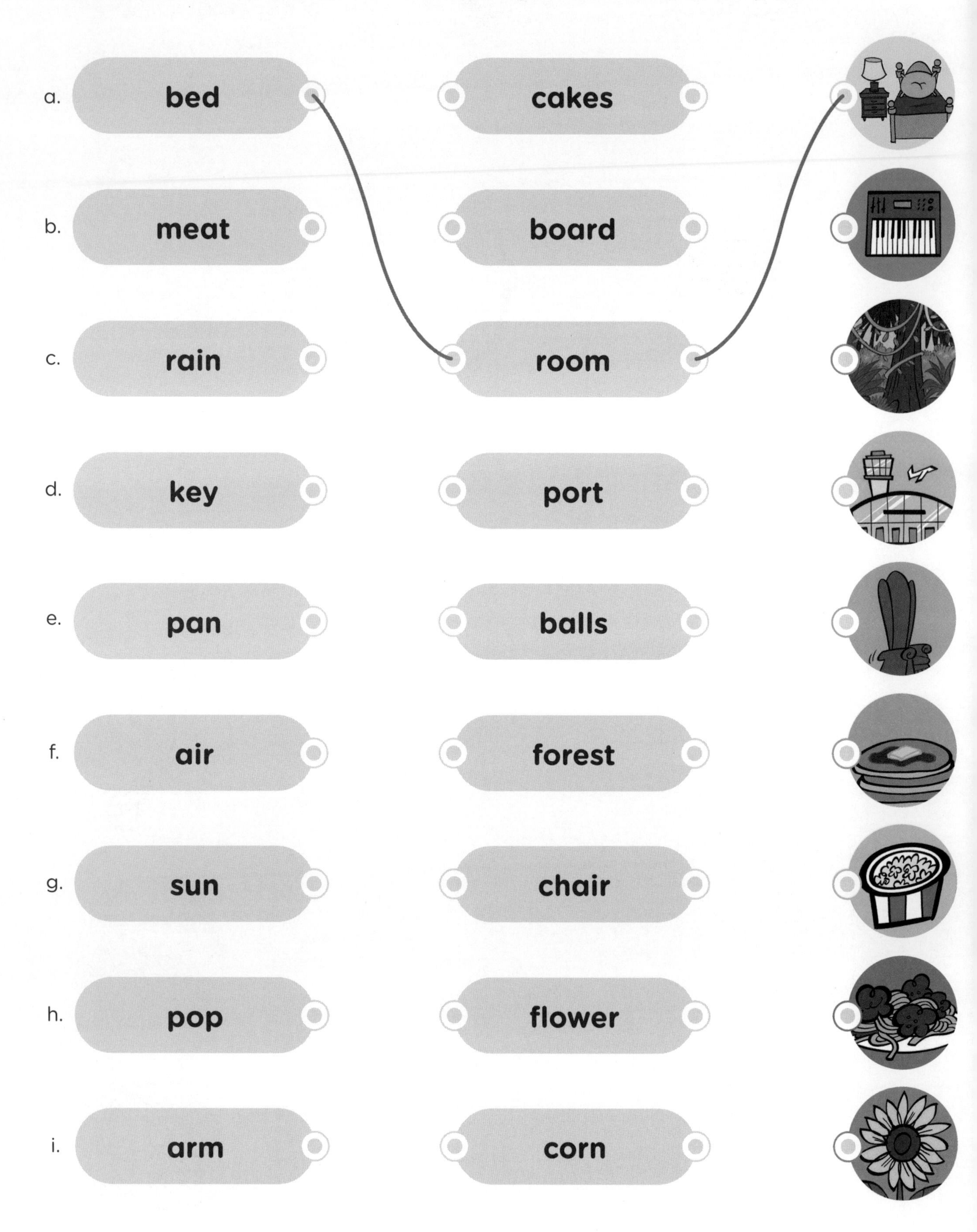

4 Underline the compound words in these sentences.

Some sentences might have more than one!

a. Bearnice was counting down the days until her next birthday.

b. Out of the window, Oz could see the snowman slowly melting in the moonlight.

c. After the football match, Yin and Yang agreed that it was time for an enormous cheeseburger and a milkshake.

d. Nobody knew how the goldfish ended up in the dishwasher.

5 Finish these compound words!

Some of the words in this text are incomplete.
Fill in the blanks using the words in the box.

boat **rain** **storm** **sun** **side**

Yin and Yang's trip to the **sea**.............................. was a disaster. Instead of beautiful, golden ....**shine** they got caught in a **thunder**.............................. . They sat under an umbrella and watched a **sail**.............................. bobbing on the waves as they listened to the sound of the ....**drops** hitting the water.

TEST YOURSELF!

What is a compound word? Answer out loud.

A synonym is a word that means the same or nearly the same as another word.

For example, **big** and **large** are synonyms.

1 Circle the synonyms.

a. Circle the synonym of **excited**.

orange **happy** **sleepy**

b. Circle the synonym of **irritated**.

annoyed **happy** **peaceful**

c. Circle the synonym of **anxious**.

relaxed **silly** **worried**

An antonym is a word that means the opposite of another word.

For example, **good** and **bad** are antonyms.

2 Draw a line to connect the antonyms.

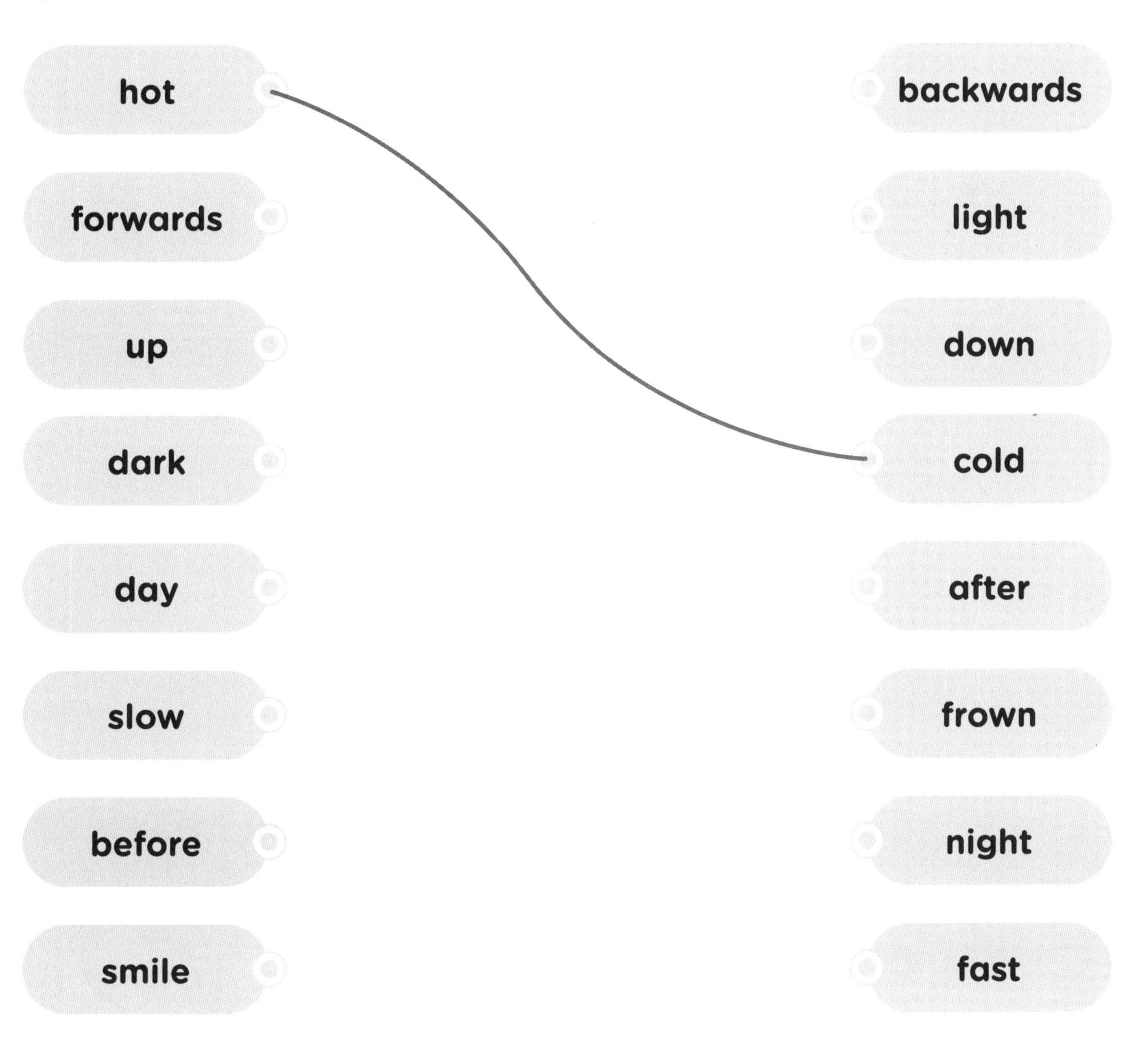

3 Identify the synonyms and antonyms.

Read through these pairs of words. Tick the synonym pairs and cross the antonym pairs.

REMEMBER!

Synonyms are words with the same or similar meanings. Antonyms are words with the opposite meanings.

- ✓ shut | close
- ✗ near | far
- giggle | laugh
- play | work
- wet | dry
- look | see
- start | finish
- sad | upset
- draw | doodle
- easy | hard
- smooth | bumpy
- love | hate
- soft | hard
- hop | jump
- quick | fast
- thin | narrow
- talk | speak
- boring | dull
- tall | short
- lost | found
- tasty | yummy

4 Write a synonym and an antonym for each word.

Use the words in the box to help you.

healthy	**yell**	**ill**	**dirty**
washed	**mean**	**nice**	**whisper**

	synonym	**antonym**
clean	....	....
shout	....	....
sick	....	....
kind	....	....

A synonym is a word that means the same
or nearly the same as another word.

Some words that have similar meanings are stronger than others.

Oz was **glad** to get a birthday present.
But she was **ecstatic** to get ten birthday presents.

The words **glad** and **ecstatic** both mean the same
as **happy**, but you might use **ecstatic** when
you are talking about being **very happy**.

EXAMPLE

heartbroken

is more sad than

upset

furious is more angry than **annoyed**

1 Which sentence uses the strongest synonym?

Read the sentences and answer the questions. These synonyms may mean the same or be similar, but one is stronger than the other.

a. Yin is upset. Yang is heartbroken.

Who is more sad? ....

b. Brick is annoyed. Bogart is furious.

Who is more angry? ....

c. Grit had a terrible day. Plato had a bad day.

Who had a worse day? ....

d. Bearnice adores doughnuts. Oz likes doughnuts.

Who likes doughnuts the most? ....

e. Oz's homework is difficult. Plato's homework is impossible.

Whose homework is harder? ....

f. Brick ate a huge slice. Oz ate a large slice. Bogart ate an enormous slice.

Who ate the biggest slice? ....

Homophones are words that **sound the same** but are **spelled differently** and have **different meanings**.

This page introduces lots of different homophones. Read through them and try to remember as many as you can.

These will help you complete the next few activities, but if you need some help, look back to this page for a reminder!

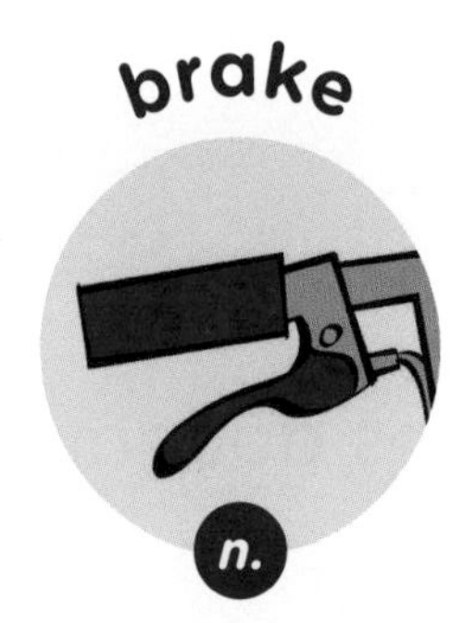

sail – The **sail** on the ship rippled in the breeze.

sale – Everything in the **sale** is half price!

two – **Two** doughnuts are better than one.

too – I ordered **too** many doughnuts!

tale – The terrible **tale** was too sad to tell.

tail – The excited puppy wagged his **tail**.

bear – The grizzly **bear** caught a fish.

bare – The cupboards were completely **bare**.

write

right

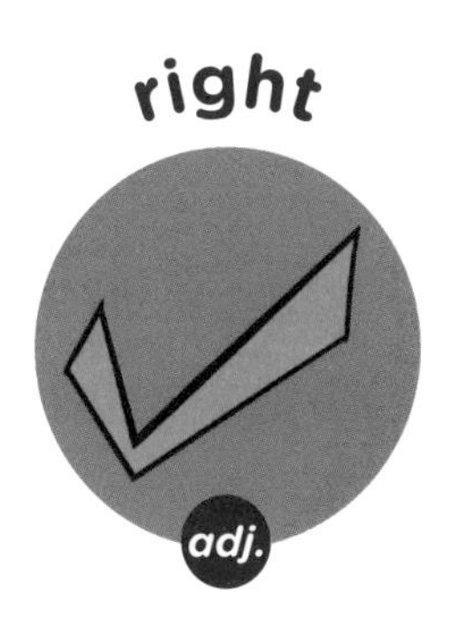

flower

flour

sun – The **sun** was high in the sky.

son – The doctor's **son** wanted to be a doctor too!

hear – Did you **hear** that noise?

here – Come **here** at once!

knight

night

mail

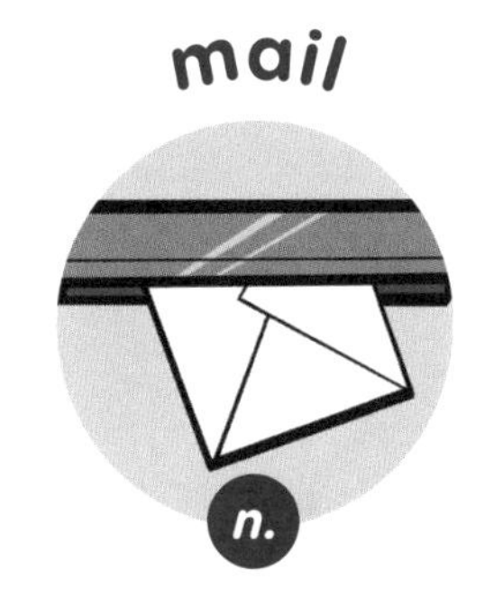

male

plane – The **plane** flew around the world.

plain – The grey furniture was very **plain**.

be – I will always **be** there for you!

bee – The **bee** flew from flower to flower.

blue

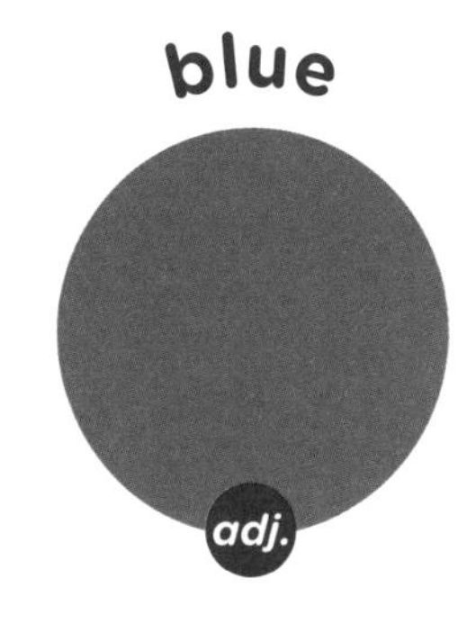

blew

1 Match the homophones to the pictures!

The words below are homophones. This means that they sound the same but are spelled differently and have different meanings. Draw a line connecting each word to the right picture.

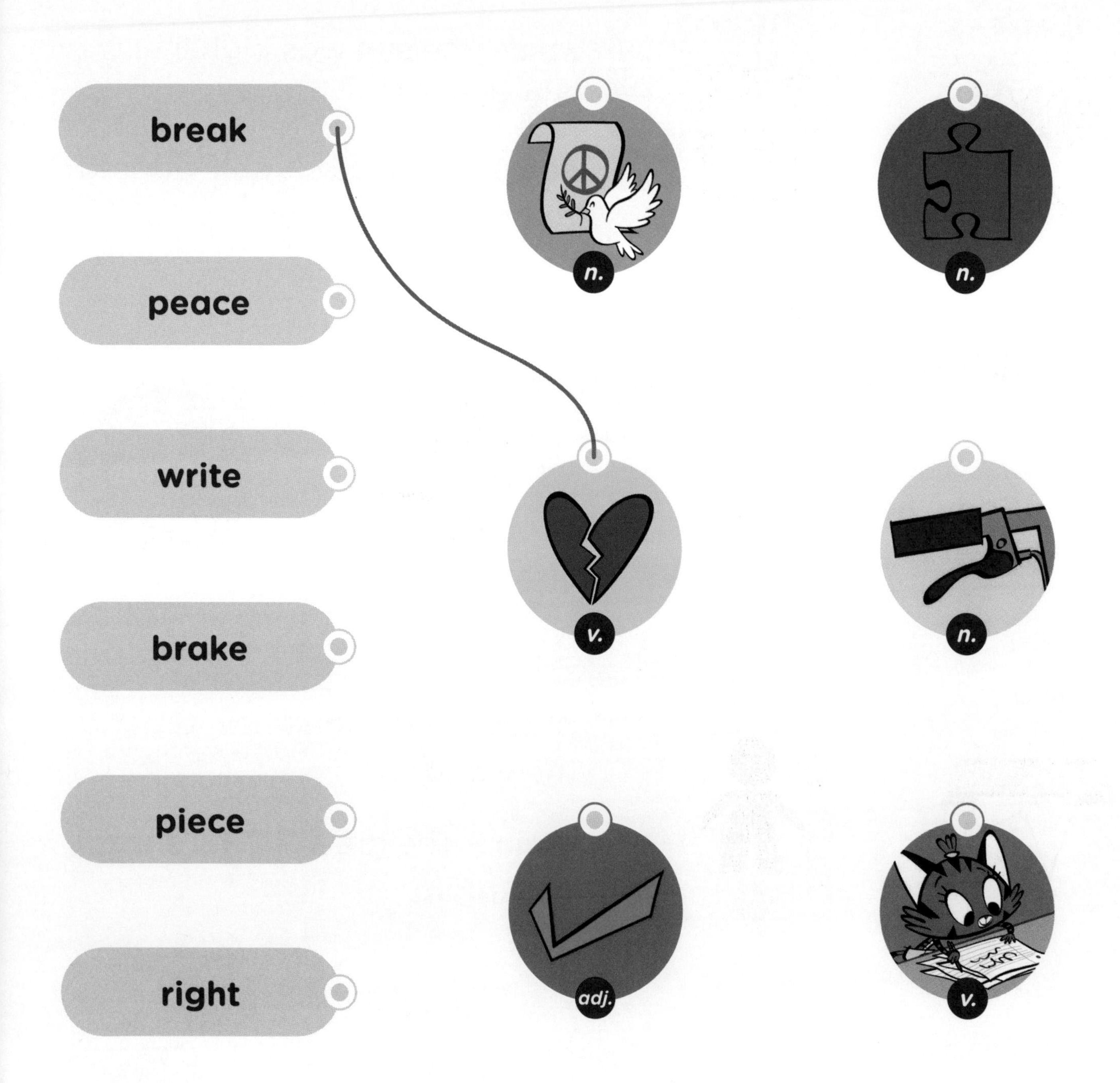

② Complete these common phrases.

The phrases below are missing a word. Can you figure out which one goes with 'peace' and which one goes with 'piece'? Draw a line connecting each word to the right picture.

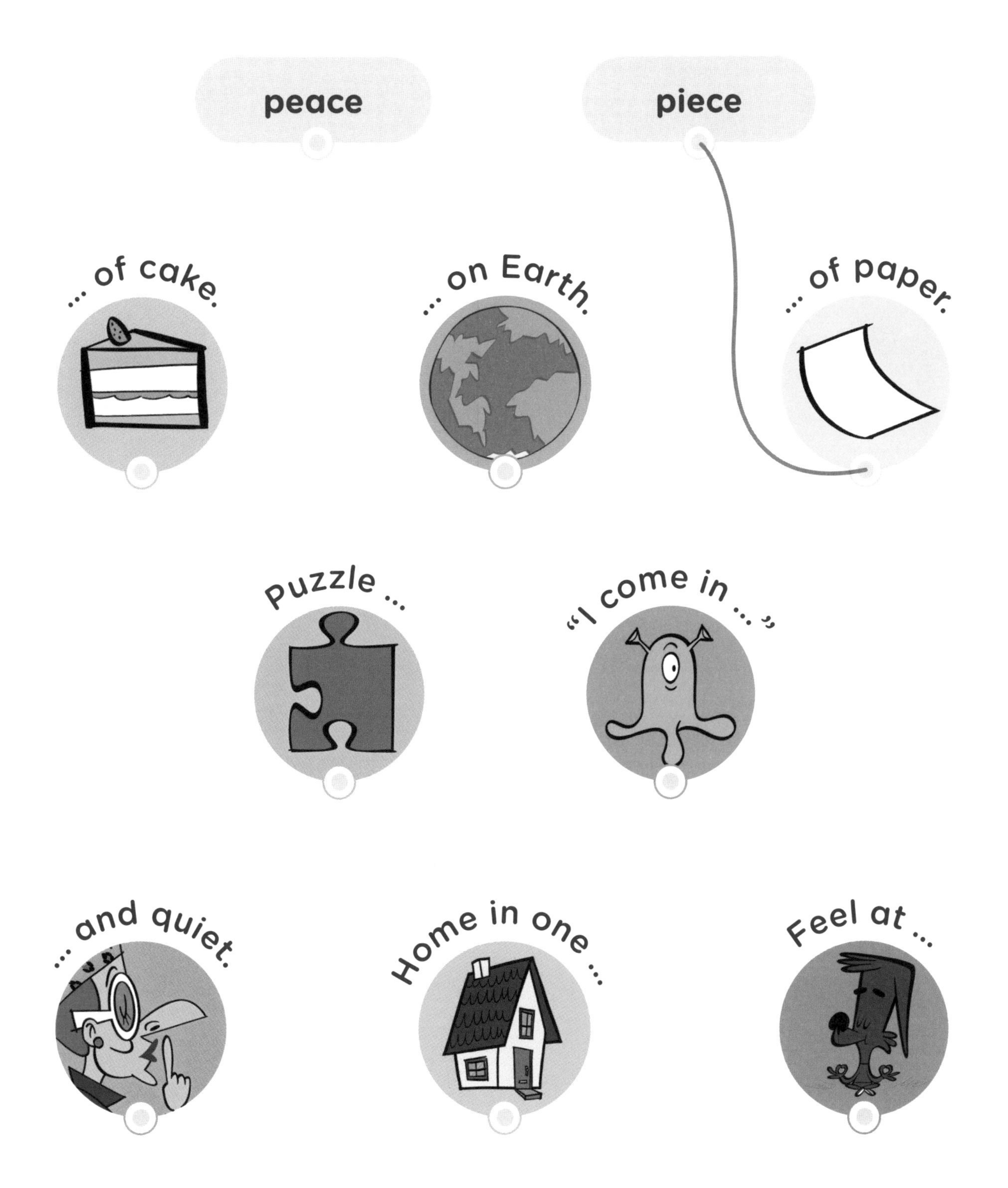

3 Circle the homophone that matches the picture.

The words below are homophones. This means that they sound the same but are spelled differently and have different meanings.

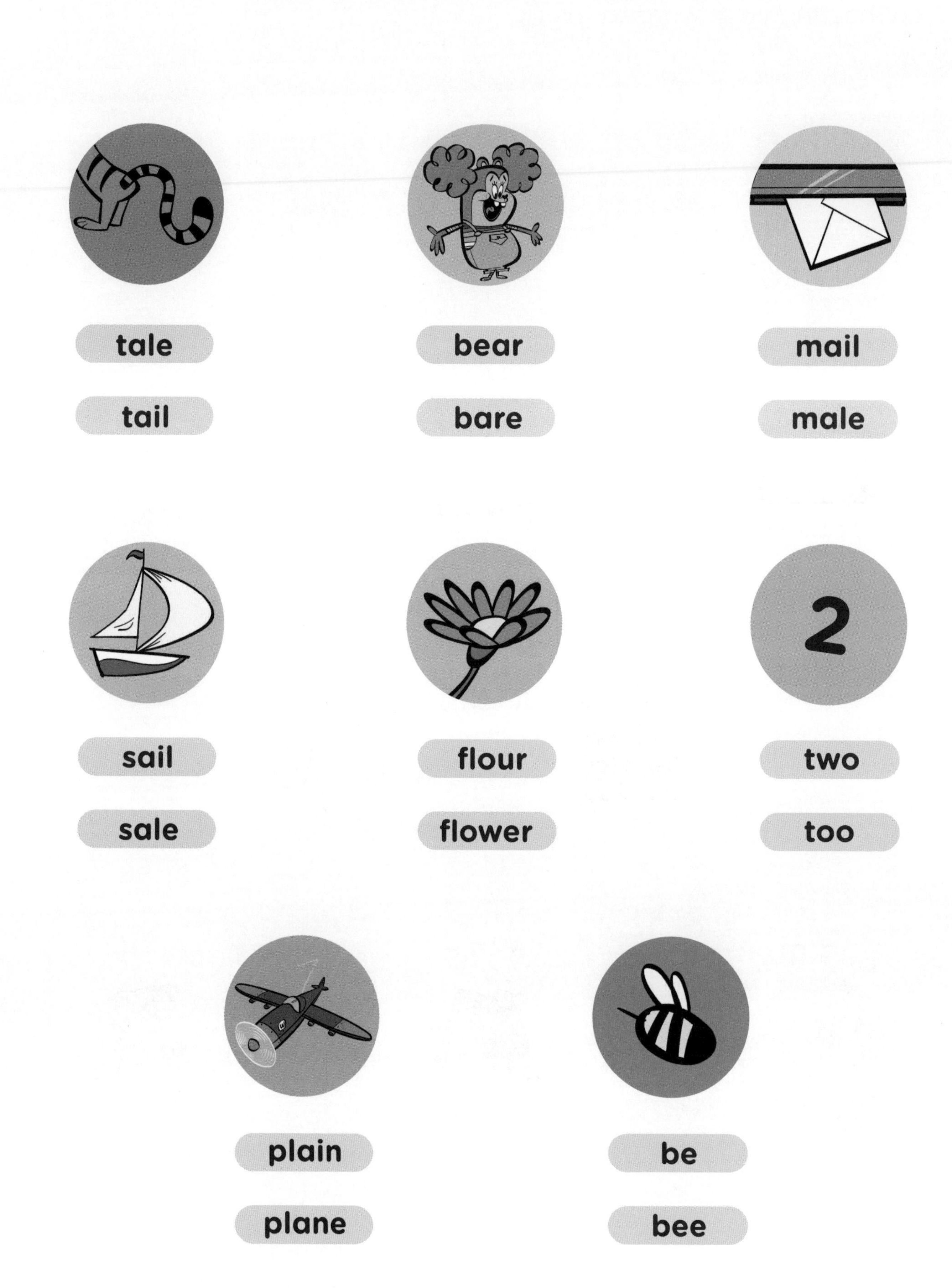

4 Complete the sentences with the correct homophone.

Choose the correct spelling and fill in the blanks.

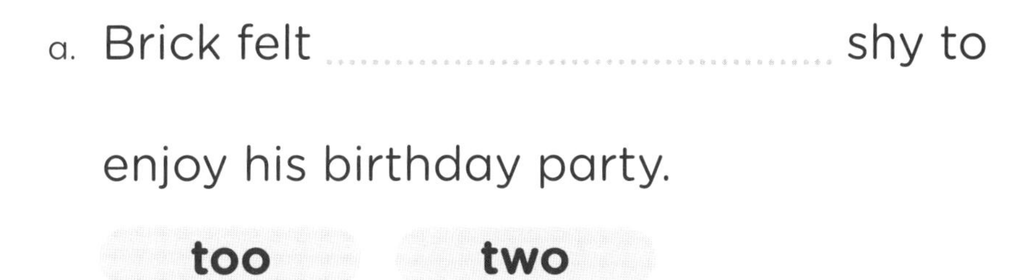

a. Brick felt .... shy to enjoy his birthday party.

too **two**

b. The .... rises in the east.

sun **son**

c. "I've lived .... all my life," said Bearnice.

hear **here**

d. Yin hates sauce and only eats .... pasta.

plane **plain**

e. If there's a new restaurant in town, Plato will .... there.

be **bee**

Multiple-meaning words are words that have the same spelling and usually sound alike, but have different meanings.

EXAMPLE

I will **park** the car next to the **park** gates.

Here, **park** means to stop a car.

Here, **park** means an outdoor space for playing.

Did you know? Multiple-meaning words are also called homonyms.

1 Spot the multiple-meaning words.

Read these sentences and underline the multiple-meaning words. Describe out loud how you can tell each meaning using the rest of the sentence as a clue (sometimes called **using context clues**).

a. Bogart left through the door on the left.

b. Yin and Yang play cards on their way to watch a play at the theatre.

c. Brick watched the rock sink to the bottom of the sink.

d. Grit liked to watch his watch, counting down the seconds until class ended.

2 Match the sentences to the correct images.

These sentences contain multiple-meaning words. Draw lines to match each sentence to the correct image.

DID YOU KNOW?

Multiple-meaning words look and sound the same, so use the context clues in the sentences to figure out their meanings.

a. The dog began to **bark**.

b. The tree **bark** was covered with ants.

c. Shang High drank a **can** of lemonade.

d. Armie **can** read anything.

e. Oz got all the answers on the test **right**.

f. At the end of the road, turn **right**.

g. Yin licked the envelope to **seal** it shut.

h. The **seal** relaxed on the beach.

SPELLING

Using the correct spelling of a word helps your reader understand exactly what you mean. In this chapter, you'll master the spellings of sounds that you might be familiar with from learning phonics. Some sounds have multiple spelling patterns and in this book you will practise the most important ones. You will also find some common exception words that don't follow the rules.

Vowel sounds can be long or short.

The sound of **a** in c**a**t is a **short a** sound.

The sound of **ai** in p**ai**nt is a **long a** sound.

EXAMPLE

The **long a** sound can be written

ai
r**ai**n

a_e
c**a**k**e**

ay
h**ay**

1 Underline the long a spelling.

Underline the letters that make the **long a** sound in each word. The first one is done for you. Then, write out each word three times.

TIP!
ai is commonly found in the middle of words and ay is commonly found at the end of words.

a. sn<u>ai</u>l ....

b. snake ....

c. play ....

2 Complete the table.

Underline the letters that make the **long a** sound in each word in the box. Then, write the words under the matching spelling pattern.

plane **tail** **holiday** **Friday** **lake**
ape **train** **mail** **say**

ai	ay	a_e
	holiday	

3 Complete these sentences.

Circle the correct spelling.

TIP!
Use the options in the box above to help you, or challenge yourself by not looking!

a. Grit wagged his **tayl** **tail** .

b. Bearnice is going on **holidaye** **holiday** .

c. Plato floated lazily across the **layk** **lake** .

d. Brick waited impatiently for his **mayl** **mail** to arrive.

e. Shang High is too tall to fly a **plane** **playn** .

f. Thank goodness it's **Friday** **Fridai** !

Vowel sounds can be long or short.

The sound of **e** in b**e**d is a **short e** sound.

The sound of **ee** in f**ee**t is a **long ee** sound.

EXAMPLES

The **long e** sound can be written

ee
like in f**ee**t

ea
like in dr**ea**m

e_e
like in athl**e**t**e**

ie
like in th**ie**f

y
like in pupp**y**

ey
like in k**ey**

1 Underline the long e spellings.

Underline the letters that make the **long e** sound in each word. The first one is done for you. Then, write out each word once.

a. geese ....
b. jeans ....
c. compete ....
d. honey ....
e. sunny ....
f. piece ....

2 Complete the table.

Underline the letters that make the **long e** sound in each word in the box. Then, write the words under the matching spelling pattern.

TIP!
y and ey are commonly found at the end of words.

geese	chimney	empty	delete	jeans	coffee
piece	thief	honey	sunny	compete	tea

ee	ea	e_e	ie	y	ey
	jeans				

3 Complete these sentences.

Fill in the missing letters using the correct **long e** spelling for each word.

TIP!
Use the options in the box above to help you, or challenge yourself by not looking!

a. Armie was chased home by angry g.........se.

b. Oz sipped her cup of t..........

c. Bogart clicked del.........t......... on the keyboard.

d. Bees make tasty hon..........

e. Yin's cookie jar was empt..........

f. Bearnice ate the last p.........ce of cake.

Vowel sounds can be long or short.

The sound of **i** in b**i**g is a **short i** sound.

The sound of **igh** in l**igh**t is a **long i** sound.

EXAMPLE

The **long i** sound can be written

igh
like in l**igh**t

i_e
like in **i**c**e**

ie
like in p**ie**

y
like in cr**y**

1 Underline the long i spelling.

Underline the letters that make the **long i** sound in each word. The first one is done for you. Then, write out each word three times.

TIP!
y is commonly found at the end of words.

a. knight ....

b. bike ....

c. lie ....

d. dry ....

2 Complete the table.

Underline the letters that make the **long i** sound in each word in the box. Then, write the words under the matching spelling pattern.

bike	why	cried	lie	knight	polite
dry	fly	fight	kite	tie	bright

igh	i_e	ie	y
knight			

TIP!
Use the options in the box above to help you, or challenge yourself by not looking!

3 Complete these sentences.

Circle the correct spelling.

a. Shang High wore his best suit and **tie** **tigh** .

b. Oz dreamed of being able to **flie** **fly** .

c. Armie is always very **polite** **polight** .

d. Yin and Yang often **fyt** **fight** .

Vowel sounds can be long or short.

The sound of **o** in h**o**t is a **short o** sound.

The sound of **oa** in s**oa**p is a **long o** sound.

EXAMPLE

The **long o** sound can be written

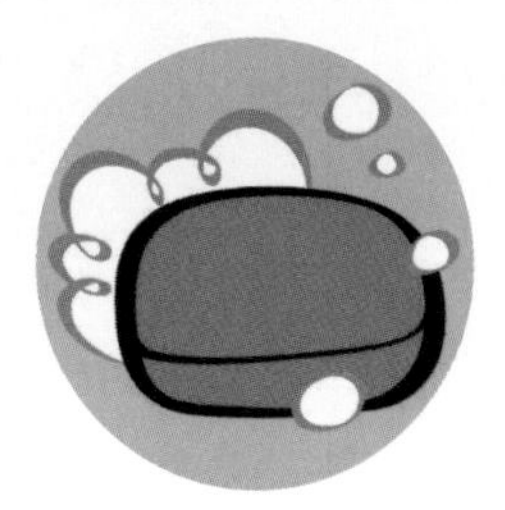

oa
like in s**oa**p

ow
like in b**ow**

o_e
like in r**o**p**e**

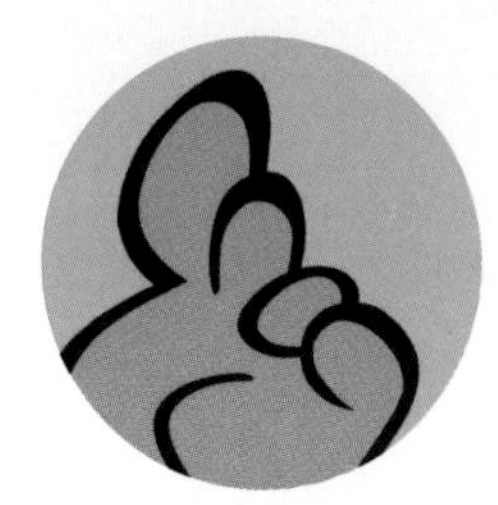

oe
like in t**oe**

1 Underline the long o spelling.

Underline the letters that make the **long o** sound in each word. The first one is done for you. Then, write out each word three times.

TIP!
ow is commonly found at the end of words.

a. toast ....

b. snow ....

c. phone ....

d. doe ....

2 Complete the table.

Underline the letters that make the **long o** sound in each word in the box. Then, write the words under the matching spelling pattern.

doe	road	slow	window	joke	phone
goal	nose	toe	toast	snow	foe

oa	ow	o_e	oe
	snow		

3 Complete these sentences.

Fill in the missing letters using the correct **long o** spelling for each word.

Use the options in the box above to help you, or challenge yourself by not looking!

a. Grit burnt his t....... ....st.

b. Yin and Yang played in the sn....... ....

c. Oz took a photo with her ph.......n....... .

d. Armie crossed the r....... ....d.

e. Shang High looked out the wind....... ....

f. Brick scored a g....... ....l.

The sound of **oo** in b**oo**k is a **short oo** sound.
The sound of **oo** in m**oo**n is a **long oo** sound.

FOR EXAMPLE:

The **long oo** sound can be written

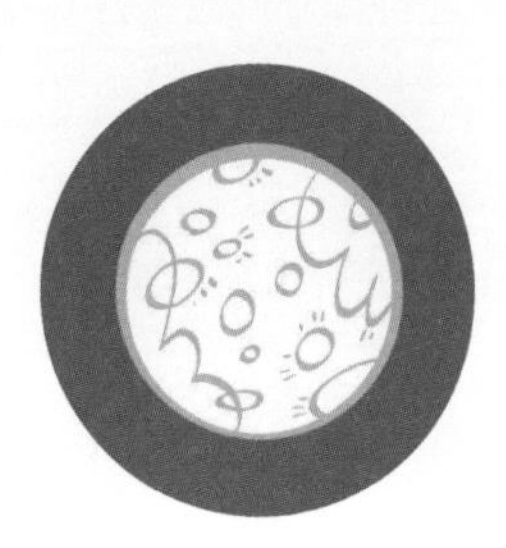

oo
like in m**oo**n

ou
like in s**ou**p

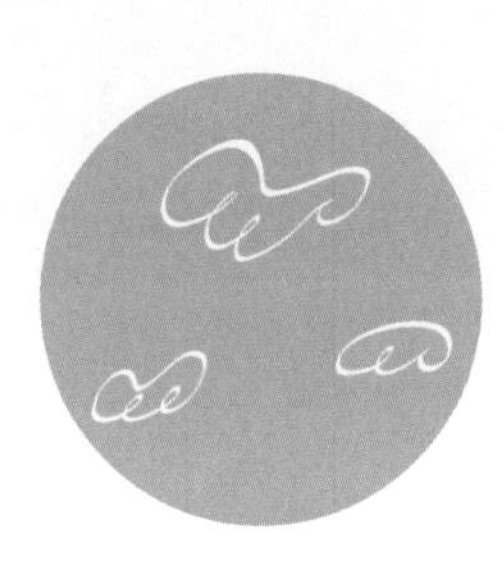

ue
like in bl**ue**

ew
like in n**ew**t

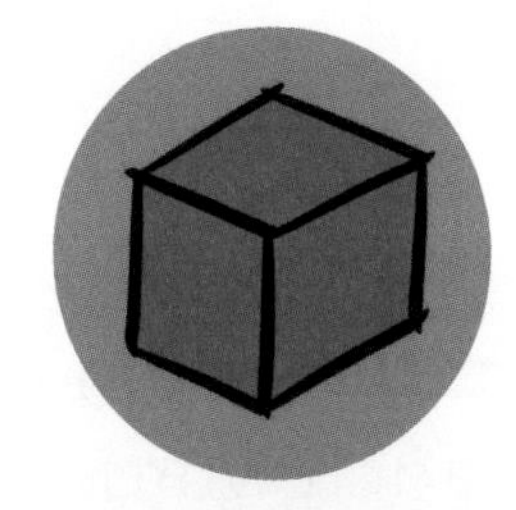

u_e
like in c**u**b**e**

1 Underline the long oo spellings.

Underline the letters that make the long oo sound in each word. Then, write out each word three times.

a. food ....

b. group ....

c. glue ....

d. stew ....

e. flute ....

2 Complete the table.

Underline the letters that make the **long oo** sound in each word in the box. Then, write the words under the matching spelling pattern.

food **statue** **glue** **roof** **flute**
chew **soup** **tune** **stew** **group**

oo	ou	ue	ew	u_e
			chew	

> TIP!
> Use the options in the box above to help you, or challenge yourself by not looking!

3 Complete these sentences.

Circle the correct spelling.

a. The world's biggest toffee took three days to **chew** **chue** .

b. Yin accidentally stuck her hands together with **glue** **glou** .

c. Bearnice hummed a happy **tewn** **tune** .

d. Plato loves all types of **fude** **food** .

e. The car was too small for the big **gruep** **group** of friends.

f. Shang High sat on the **rouf** **roof** to watch the sunset.

1 Match the word to the correct oo sound.

Draw lines to connect each word to the type of oo sound it makes. Say the words out loud to help you.

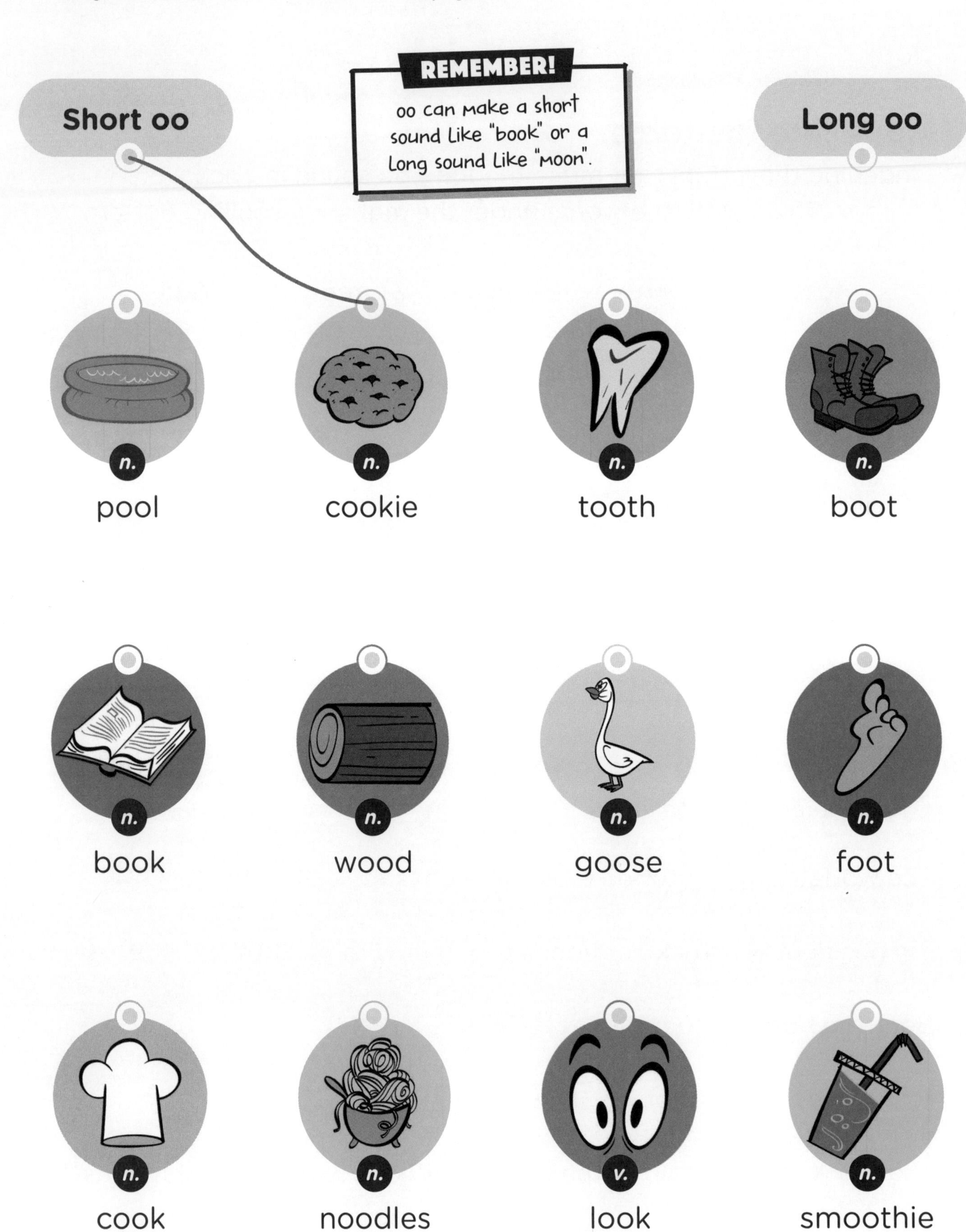

1 Match the word to the correct ea sound.

Draw lines to connect each word to the type of ea sound it makes. Say the words out loud to help you.

The **short o** sound can be written with an **o**, like in p**o**t and b**o**x.

But when the **short o** sound comes after **qu** or **w**, it is written with an **a**, like in w**a**tch and qu**a**lity.

1 Underline the short o spellings.

Can you underline the letter that makes the **short o** sound in each word? Write out each word twice to practise.

REMEMBER!
These can be tricky because they're spelled differently to how they sound.

a.

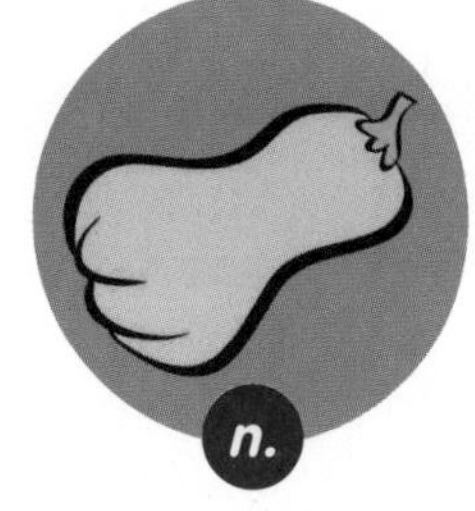

n.

squash

....

....

b.

n.

watch

....

....

c.

n.

swan

....

....

d.

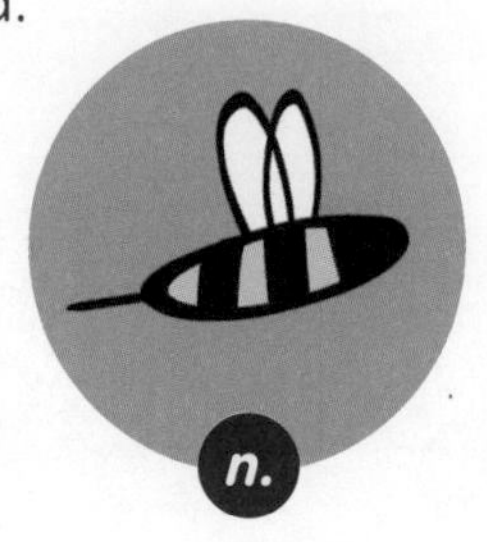

n.

wasp

....

....

e.

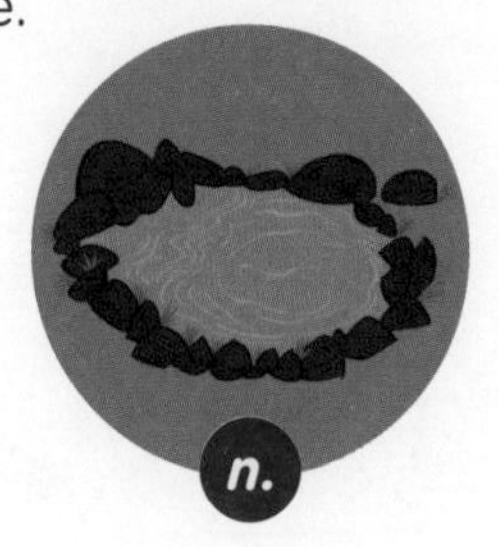

n.

swamp

....

....

f.

n.

wand

....

....

2 Underline the words that are spelled correctly.

All these words have a **short o** sound, but remember, this is written as **a** after **qu** or **w**.

what / whot	**wosp / wasp**	**quality / quolity**
wosh / wash	**squat / squot**	**swomp / swamp**

3 Complete these sentences.

Fill in the missing letters using the correct **short o** spelling for each word. Remember to watch out for **qu** and **w**!

a. Oz waved her magic w ... nd.

b. Armie turned the key to l ... ck the door.

c. Yin and Yang always qu ... rrel.

d. Brick has very smelly s ... cks.

e. Bogart really w ... nts to take over the world.

f. "St ... p!" shouted Bearnice.

g. Plato sw ... llowed the pizza whole,

and now he w ... nts more!

The **short u** sound can be written with a **u**,
like in m**u**d and d**u**ck.

But the **short u** sound can also be written with an **o**.
This is often the case when the **short u**,
comes before **v**, **n** or **th**, like in l**o**ve.

1 Underline the short u spellings.

Can you underline the letter that makes the **short u** sound in each word? Write out each word three times to practise.

REMEMBER!
These can be tricky because they're spelled differently to how they sound.

a. month ....

b. brother ....

c. oven ....

2 Complete these words.

Fill in the missing letters using the correct **short u** spelling for each word. Remember, **short u** is usually written as **o** before **v**, **n** or **th**.

a.

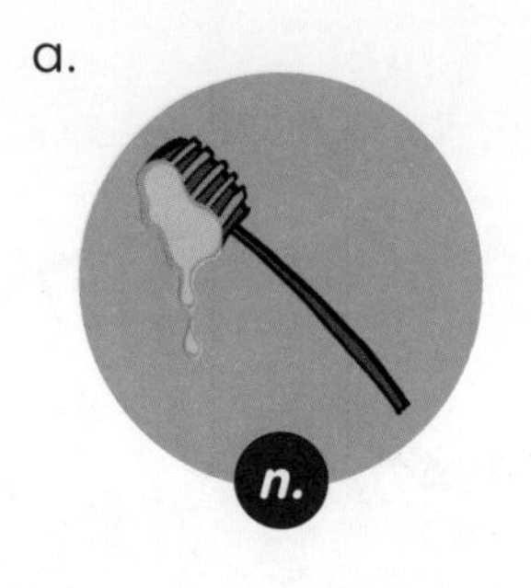

h ... ney

b.

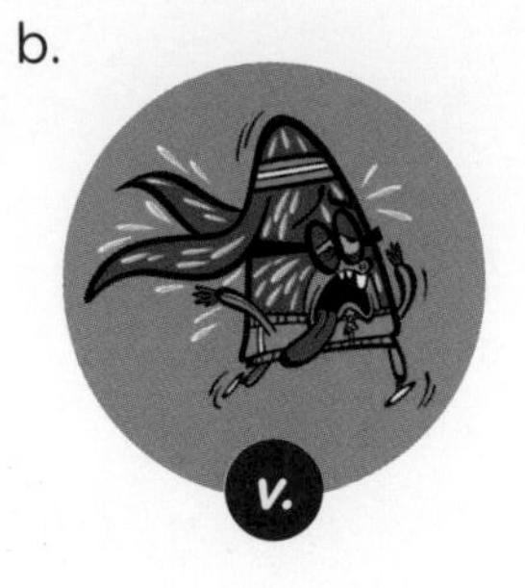

r ... sh

c.

m ... nkey

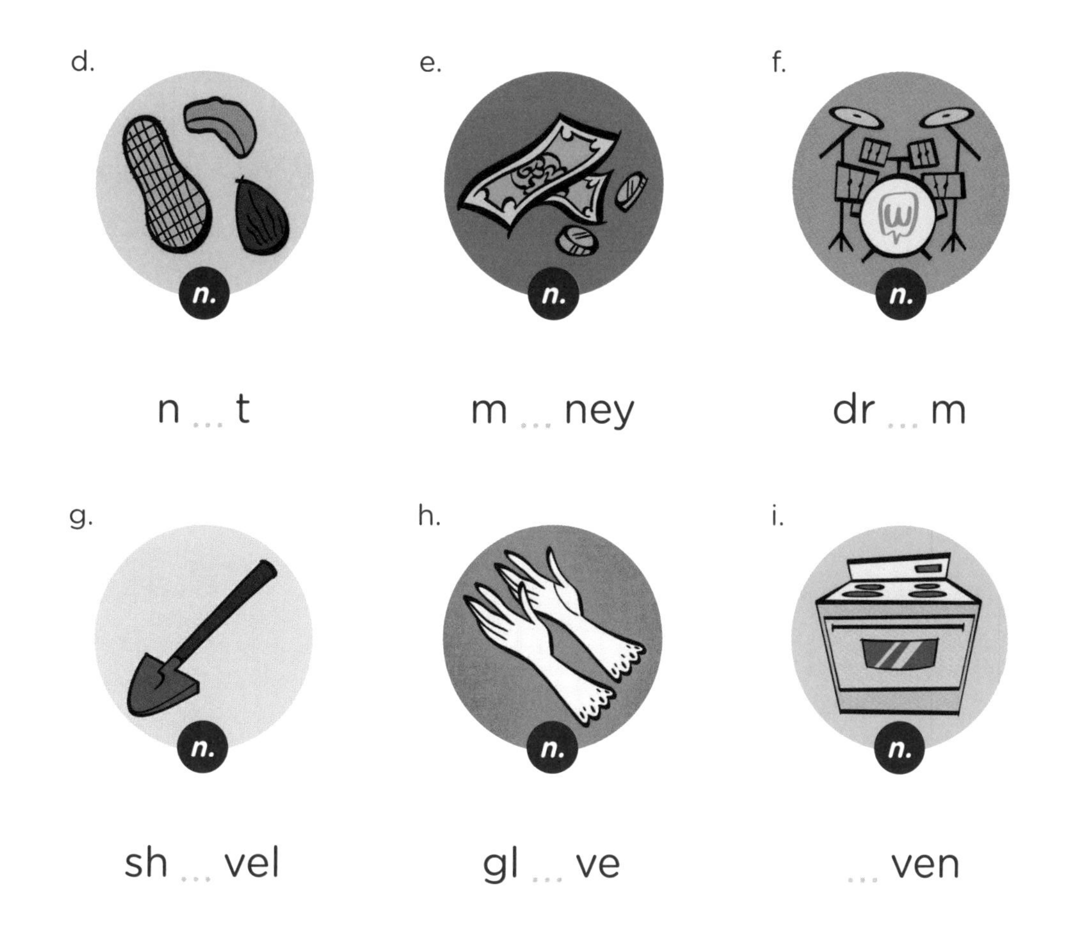

3 Complete these sentences.

Circle the correct spelling. Remember to watch out for **v**, **n** or **th**!

a. Yang **jumped** **jomped** in muddy puddles.

b. Bogart filled Brick's **gloves** **gluves** with custard.

c. Grit hates **Mondays** **Mundays** !

d. Plato baked a **plum** **plom** pie.

e. **Nothing** **Nuthing** could stop Oz from winning.

f. Bearnice chews a lot of **gom** **gum** .

g. Brick used a **shuvel** **shovel** to clear the snow.

h. Yin and Yang love each **uther** **other** .

The **aw** sound can be written with an **aw**, like in p**aw**.

When the **aw** sound is before an **l** or **ll**, it is written with an **a**, like in t**a**lk or c**a**ll.

When the **aw** sound is after a **w**, it is written with an **ar**, like in w**ar**t.

1 Underline the aw sound spellings.

Can you underline the letter(s) that makes the **aw sound** in each word? Write out each word three times to practise.

REMEMBER!
These can be tricky because they're spelled differently to how they sound.

a. draw ....

b. small ....

c. warm ....

2 Complete these words.

Fill in the missing letters using the correct **aw** spelling.
Remember, the **aw sound** can be written **aw**, **a** (before **l** or **ll**).

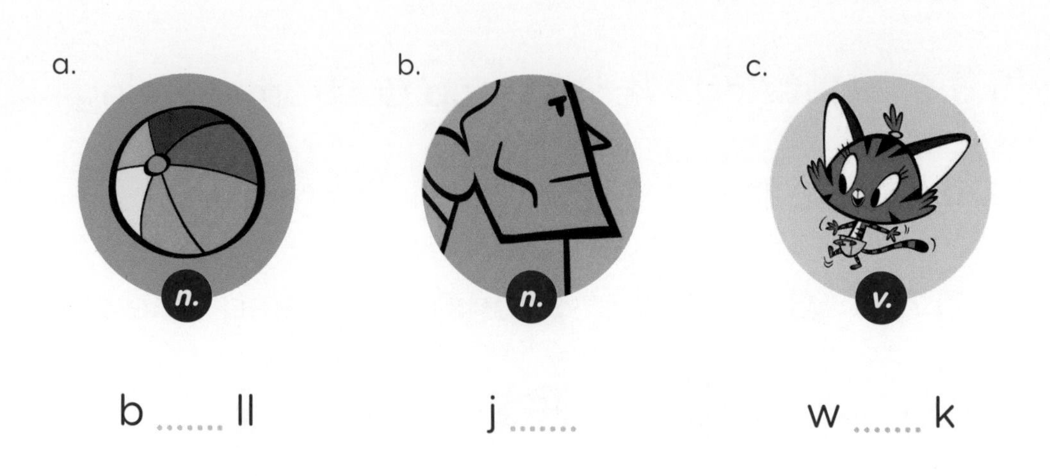

b ll   j ....   w .... k

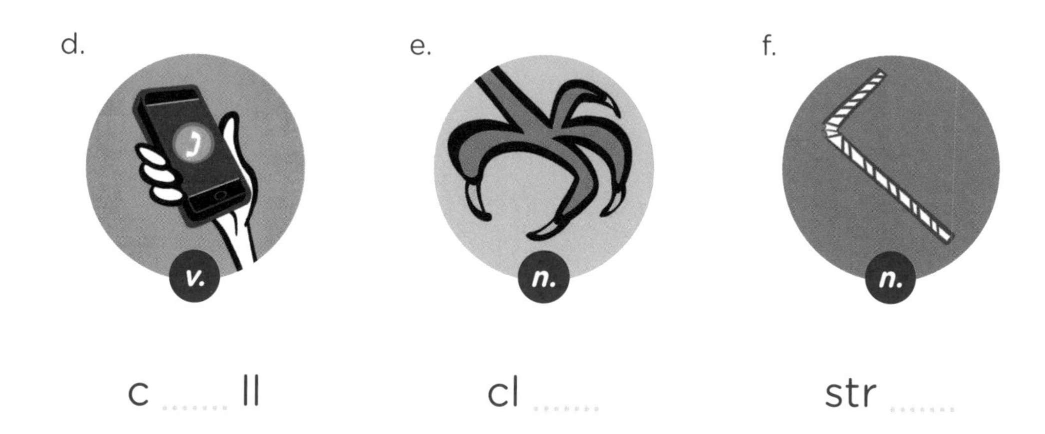

c ll   cl ....   str ....

3 Complete these sentences.

Choose the correct spelling and fill in the blanks.

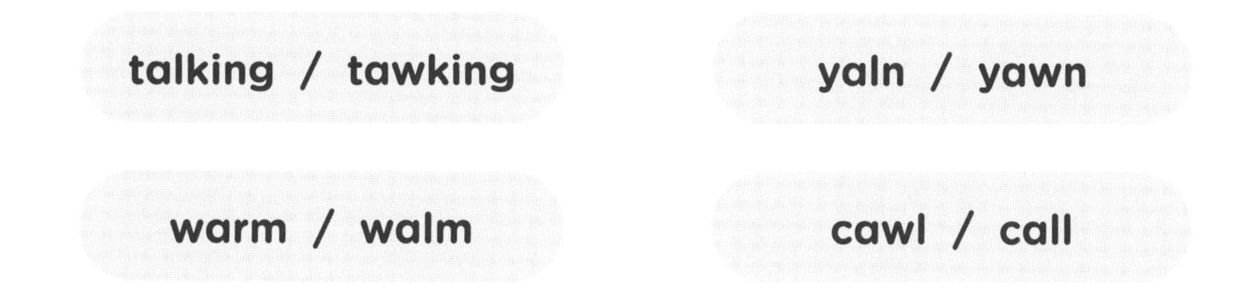

a. Pick up a phone and .... me!

b. What on Earth are you .... about?

c. It gets very .... here in the summer.

d. When I'm tired, I .... constantly.

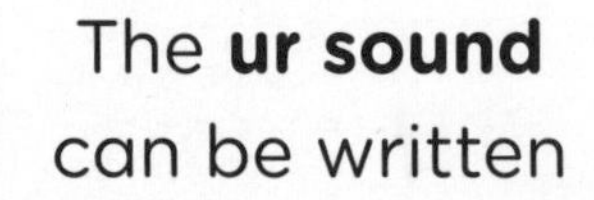

The **ur sound** can be written

ur
like in s**ur**f

ir
like in b**ir**d

er
like in g**er**m

After a **w**, the **ur** sound is written

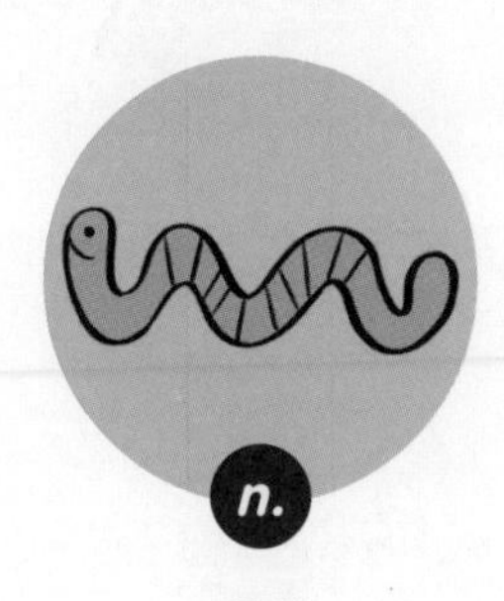

or
like in w**or**m

 1 Underline the ur sound spellings.

Underline the letters that make the **ur** sound in each word. The first one is done for you. Then, write out each word twice.

a.

h**ur**t

....

....

b.

circus

....

....

c.

hammer

....

....

d.

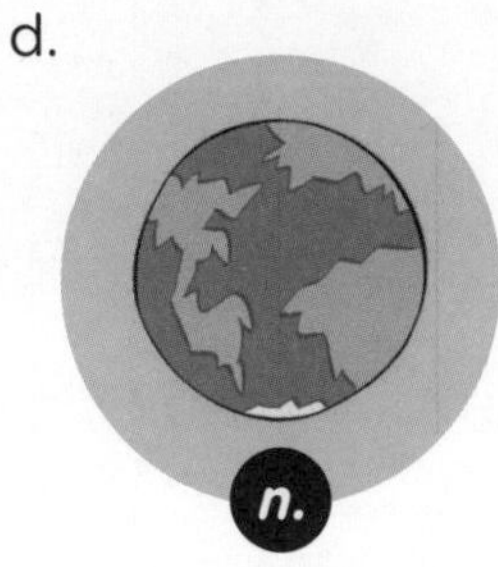

world

....

....

2 Complete the table.

Underline the letters that make the **ur** sound in each word in the box. Then, write the words under the matching spelling pattern.

worse	**thirsty**	**burp**	**hammer**
curly	**birthday**	**herd**	**world**

ur	ir	er	or
burp			

3 Complete these sentences.

Choose the correct spelling and fill in the blanks.

TIP!
Use the words in previous questions to help you, or challenge yourself by not looking!

thorsty / thirsty **herd / hird** **worse / wurse**

birthday / burthday **borped / burped** **curly / cirly**

a. Grit's day went from bad to ....

b. Three days without water made Brick very ....

c. The .... of cows followed Plato home.

d. Bearnice loved her .... hair.

e. Oz .... loudly after eating her lunch.

f. Bogart invited everyone to his .... party.

The **hard c** sound can be written in three different ways.

c	k	ck
c - usually found at the start or middle of a word, like in **c**up	**k** - found at the start, middle or end of a word, like in **k**ite	**ck** - usually found at the end of a word, like in so**ck**

1 Complete the table.

Underline the letters that make the **hard c** sound in each word in the box. Then, write the words under the matching spelling pattern.

sick **keyboard** **coat** **fork** **car** **duck**
park **camel** **candle** **milk** **lick** **rock**

c	k	ck
car		

2 Circle the words that are spelled correctly.

a. kar / car

b. milk / milc

c. camel / kamel

DID YOU KNOW?

If the hard c sound comes before the vowels i, e or y, the hard c is written with a k.

d. **roc** / **rock**

e. **coat** / **koat**

f. **candle** / **kandle**

The **hard c** sound is often written **k** or **ck** at the end of words. Whether **k** or **ck** is used depends on the sound of the vowel.

Words that have a **short vowel** sound before the **hard c** end with **ck**, like so**ck**.

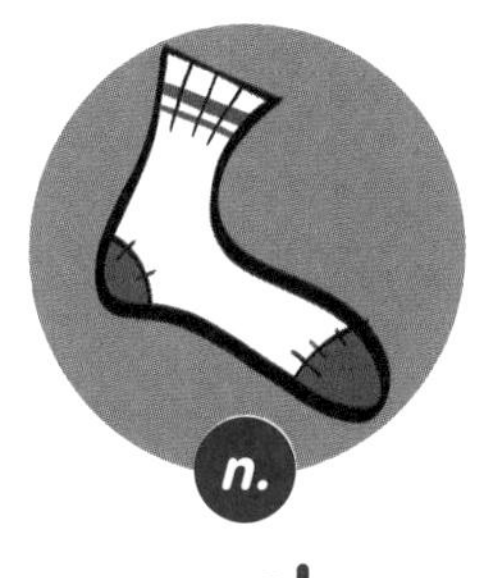

so**ck**

Words that have a **long vowel sound** before the **hard c** end with **k**, like chee**k**.

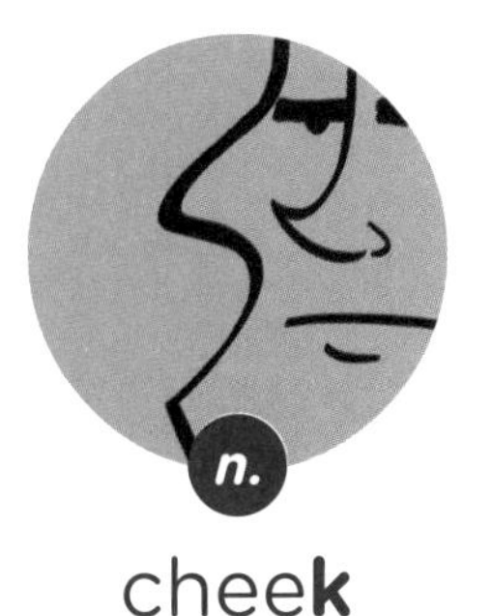

chee**k**

3 Complete these sentences.

Circle the correct spelling. Remember to watch out for long or short vowel sounds!

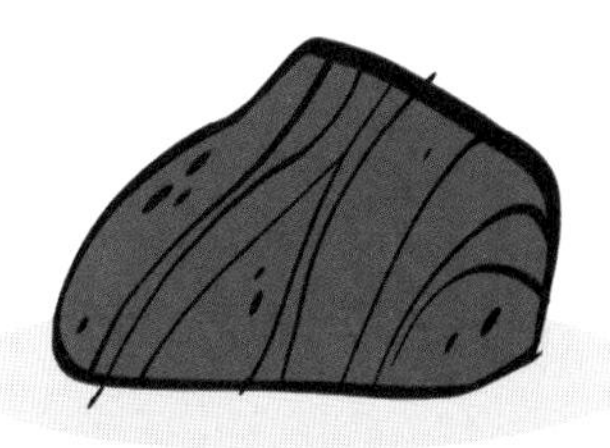

a. Yang drinks a lot of **milk** **milck** .

b. Grit stubbed his toe on a **rok** **rock** .

c. Yin and Yang play the **keyboard** **ceyboard** .

d. Eating eight cakes made Plato feel **sik** **sick** .

e. Bearnice wore her favourite red **coat** **koat** .

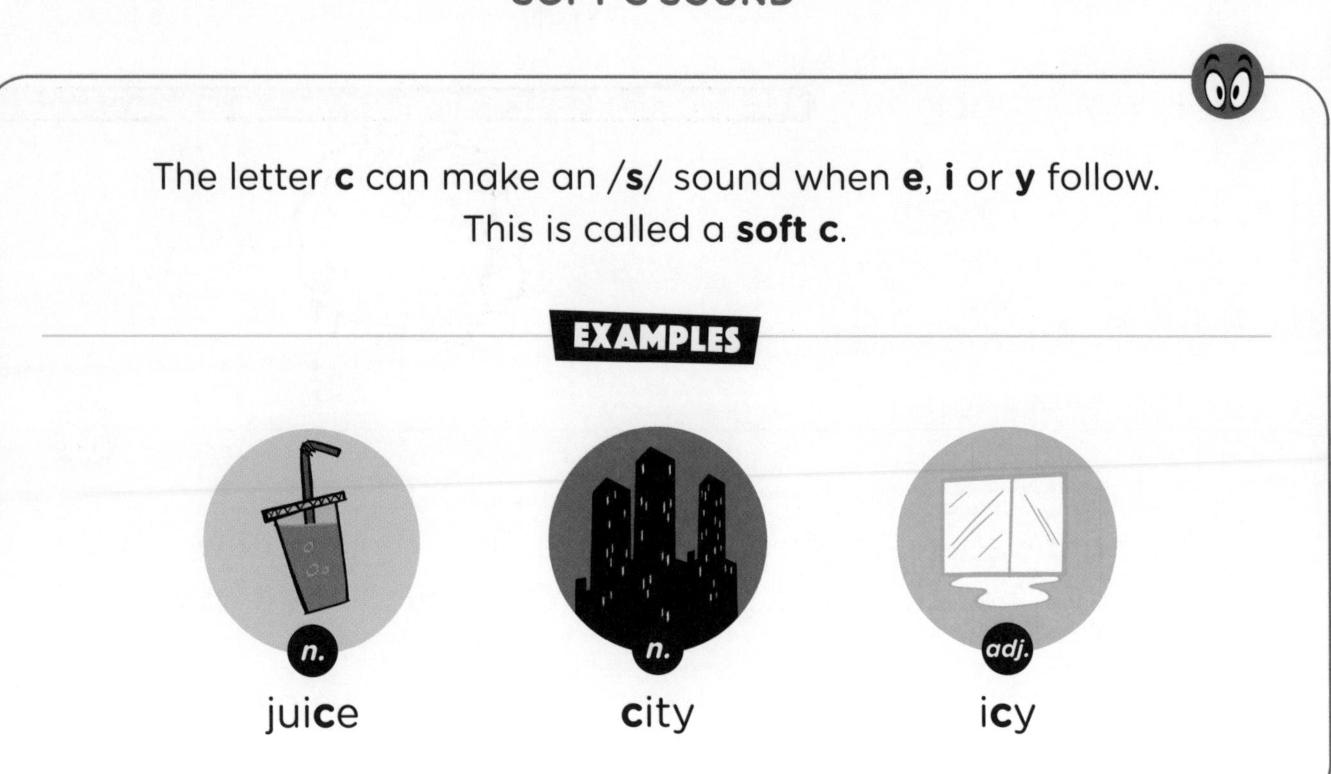

The letter **c** can make an /**s**/ sound when **e**, **i** or **y** follow. This is called a **soft c**.

EXAMPLES

1 Complete these sentences.

Fill in the blanks with the missing words.

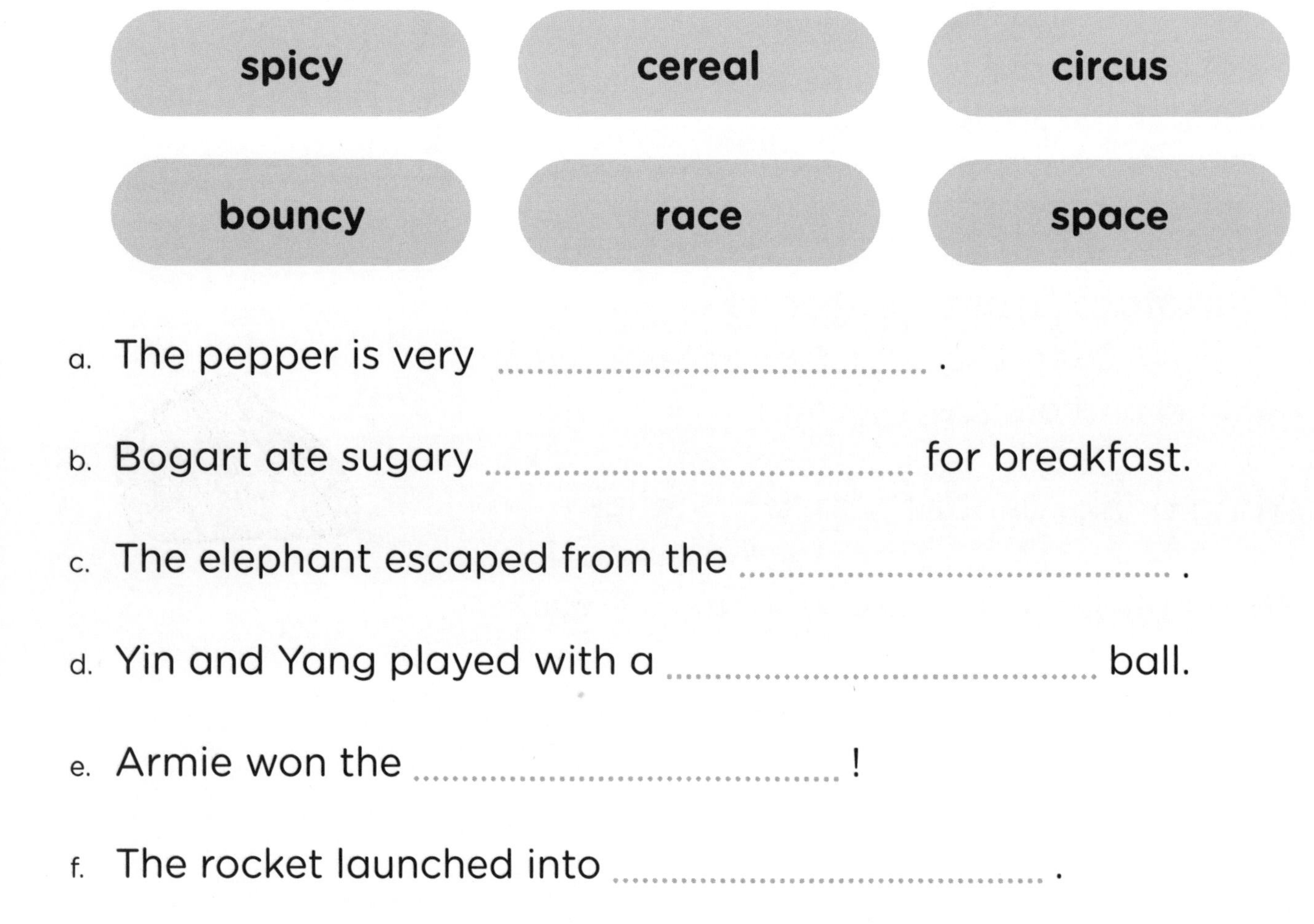

spicy **cereal** **circus**

bouncy **race** **space**

a. The pepper is very ....

b. Bogart ate sugary .... for breakfast.

c. The elephant escaped from the ....

d. Yin and Yang played with a .... ball.

e. Armie won the .... !

f. The rocket launched into ....

2 Circle the words that are spelled correctly.

Remember, the letter **c** makes an /**s**/ sound when **e**, **i** or **y** follow!

a. **fase** / **face**

b. **spider** / **cpider**

c. **mise** / **mice**

d. **snake** / **cnake**

e. **voise** / **voice**

3 Complete these words.

Fill in the gaps with **s** or **c** for each word.
Remember to watch out for **e**, **i** and **y**!

a.

ri ... e

b.

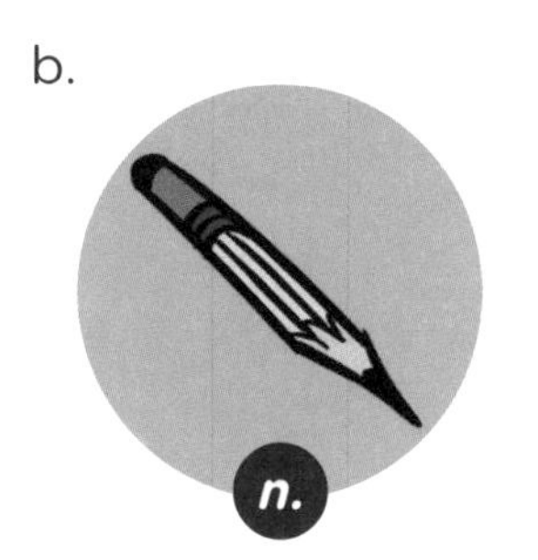

pen ... il

c.

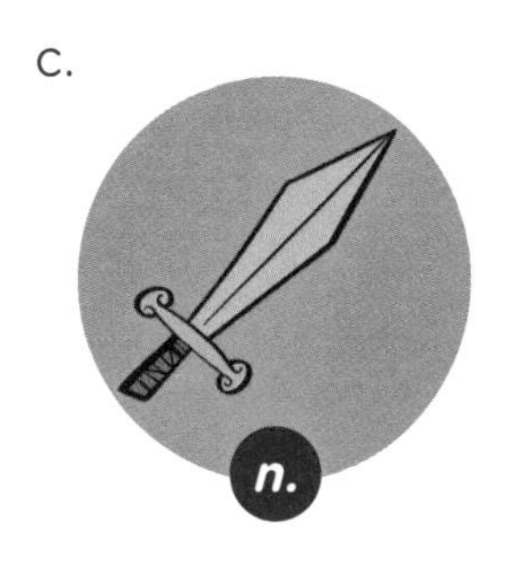

... word

d.

... inema

e.

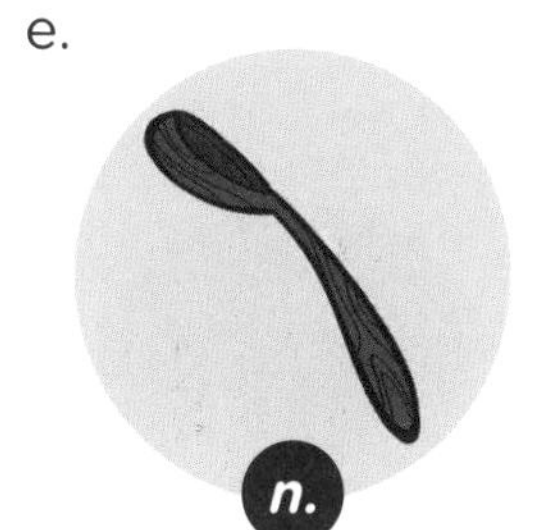

... poon

f.

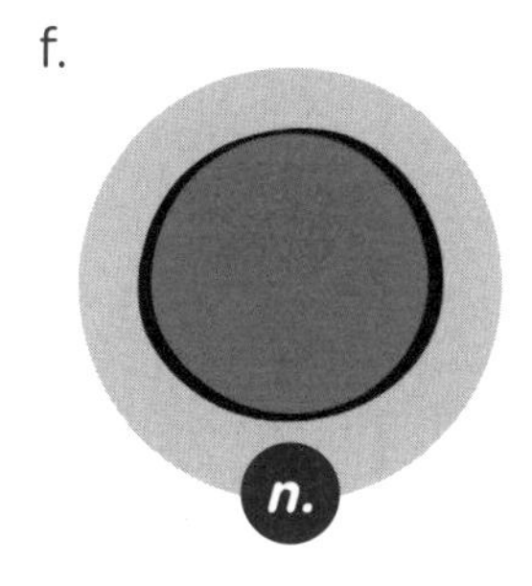

... ircle

g.

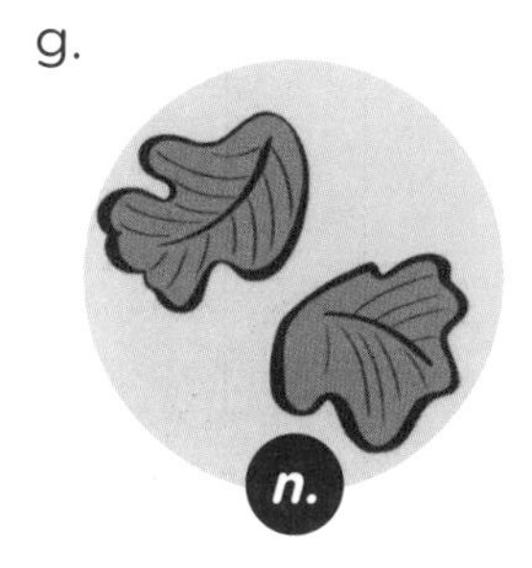

lettu ... e

h.

... ock

Soft g is the sound in words like **g**iraffe and **j**am.

Soft g can be found at the beginning, middle or end of a word. At the beginning or middle of a word, it is written as **g** like **g**iraffe or **j** like **j**am. At the end of a word, it is written as **ge** like oran**ge** or **dge** like bri**dge**.

1 Complete the table.

Underline the letters that make the **soft g** sound in each word in the box. Then, write the words under the matching spelling pattern.

jam **badge** **jigsaw** **cage** **giant**
sledge **stage** **hedge** **gem** **giraffe** **bridge**
magic **jog** **page** **huge** **jail**

g	j	ge	dge
	jam		

2 Complete these words.

Fill in the gaps with **j** or **dge** for each word.

a.

ba ....

b.

.... og

c.

.... am

d.

.... ail

3 Complete these words.

Fill in the gaps with **g** or **ge** for each word.

a.

pa ....

b.

ca ....

c.

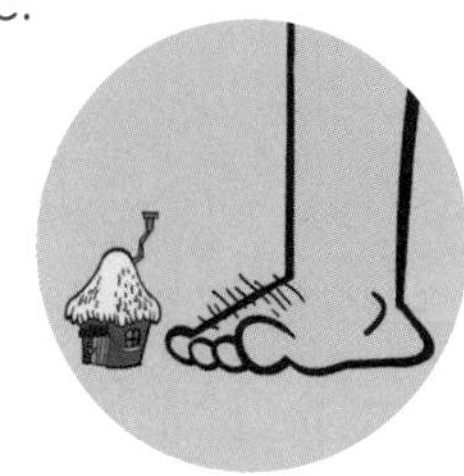

.... iant

d.

.... em

e.

.... iraffe

f.

ma ic

4 Complete these sentences.

Fill in the gaps with **j**, **dge**, **g** or **ge** for each word.

a. Yin and Yang slid down the snowy hill on a sle ....

b. Bogart is tiny and Shang High is hu ....

c. Oz loved to perform on sta ....

d. Armie finished his .... igsaw puzzle.

Sometimes, letters can get very shy.
When they're feeling shy, they don't make a sound.

The letters **k** and **g** are very shy
in front of the letter **n**. They are silent.

At the start of words, the letter **w** is very shy
in front of the letter **r**. It is silent.

EXAMPLES

knee

gnaw

wrap

1 Circle the words where the k, g or w is silent.

gnome | goose | worry

gnat | write

kind | wear

know | kneel

2 Complete these words.

Fill in the missing letters with either **kn** or **wr** for each word.

a.

.... ight

b.

.... ist

c.

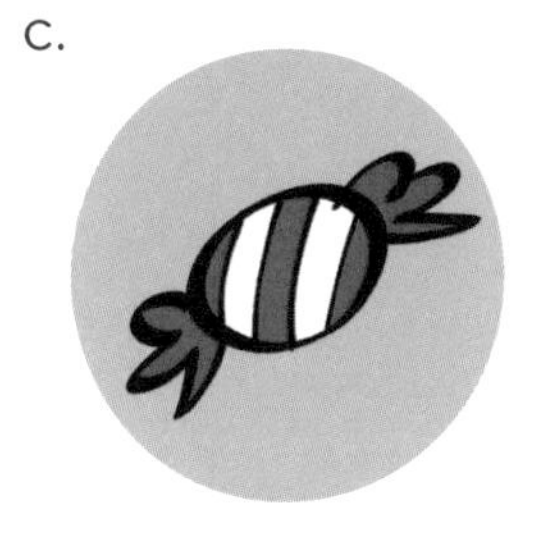

.... apper

d.

.... ife

e.

.... ite

f.

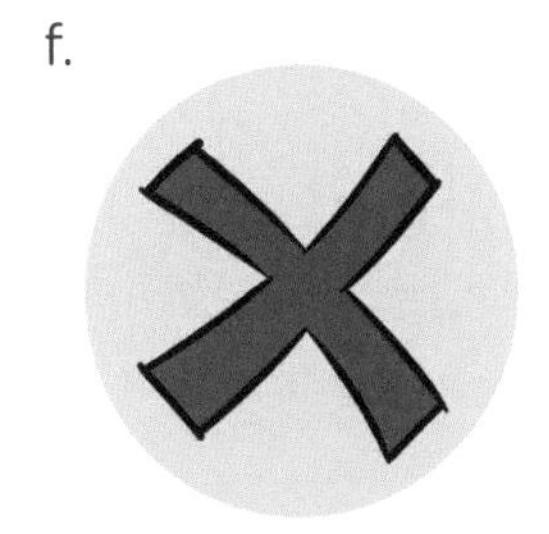

.... ong

3 Complete these sentences.

Circle the correct spelling.

a. Oz cut her birthday cake with a **wrife** **knife** .

b. A fly sat on the end of Oz's **nose** **gnose** .

c. Yin **grote** **wrote** a letter to Yang.

d. There was **nothing** **wrothing** inside the treasure chest.

e. The **rabbit** **knabbit** ate a carrot.

f. Grit saved the day like a brilliant **knight** **gnight** .

Some words can end in the same sound, but with different spellings. The endings **-el**, **-le**, **-al** and **-il** often sound the same.

FOR EXAMPLE:

ang**el**

met**al**

penc**il**

turt**le**

1 Circle the words that end in the same sound.

fridge **pupil** **freckle** **umbrella**

2 Complete the table.

Underline the ending **-el**, **-le**, **-al** or **-il** in each word in the box. Then, write the words under the matching spelling pattern.

tunnel **hospital** **fossil** **castle** **middle**
towel **animal** **nostril** **simple**
pupil **level** **sandal**

-el	-le	-al	-il
		hospital	

3 Complete these words.

a.

sand.............

b.

cast.............

c.

tunn.............

d.

hospit.............

e.

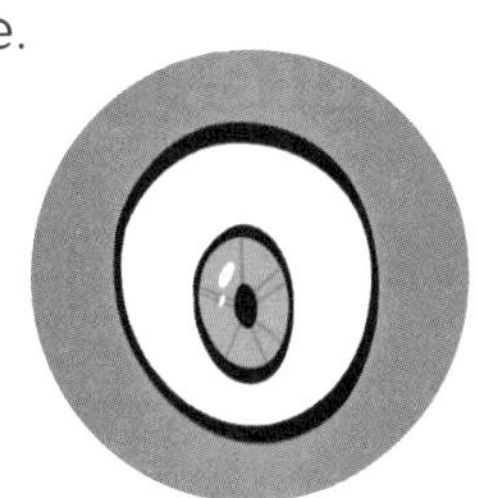

pup.............

f.

nostr.............

g.

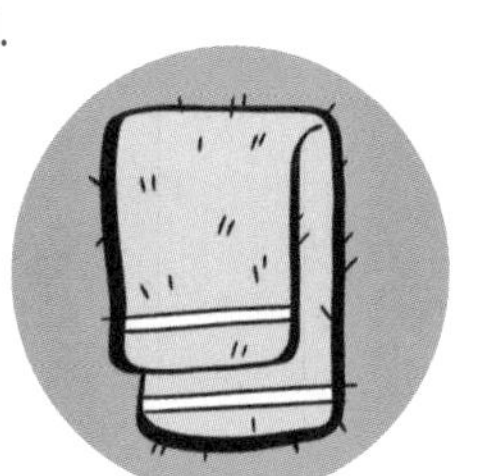

tow.............

h.

foss.............

4 Complete these sentences.

Circle the correct spelling.

a. Armie followed a **simple** **simpil** recipe.

b. Oz completed the final **levle** **level** of her game.

c. Bearnice sat in the **middal** **middle** of the field.

d. Plato found a **fossel** **fossil** in his garden.

e. Armie, Grit and Oz are different types of **animals** **animils** .

Words ending in the sound **shun** can be written **tion**.

lo**tion**

1 Complete the words and match them to a picture.

Add the suffix -**tion** to complete these words.
Write each completed word next to its matching picture.

reflec	**invita**	**educa**	**sta**
emo	**competi**	**ques**	**celebra**
ac	**pollu**	**injec**	**medita**

a.

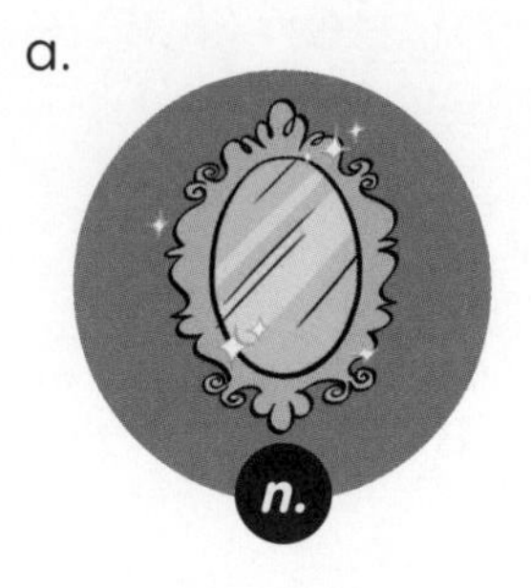

....

b.

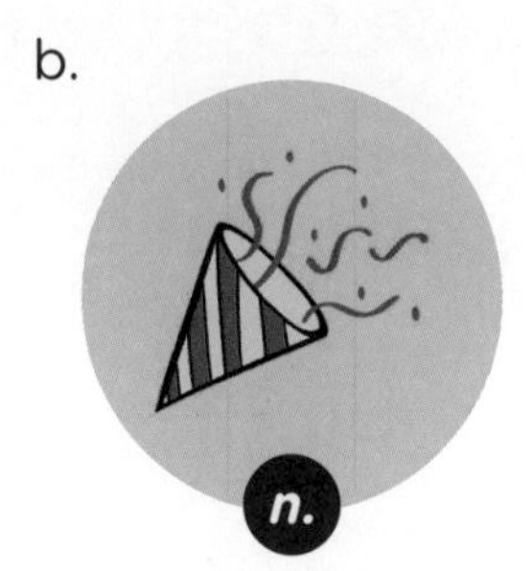

....

c.

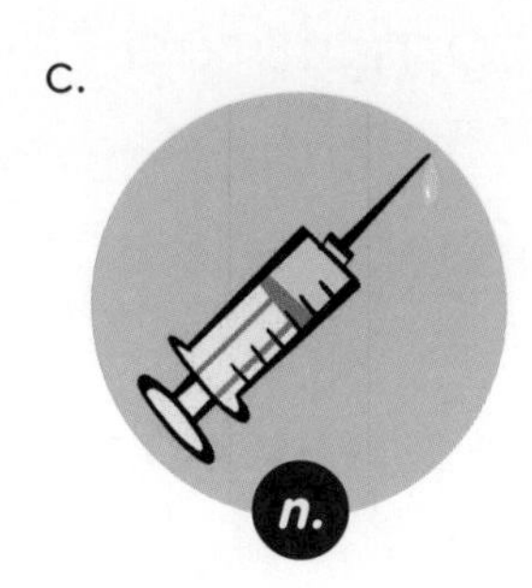

....

d.

e.

f.

g.

h.

i.

j.

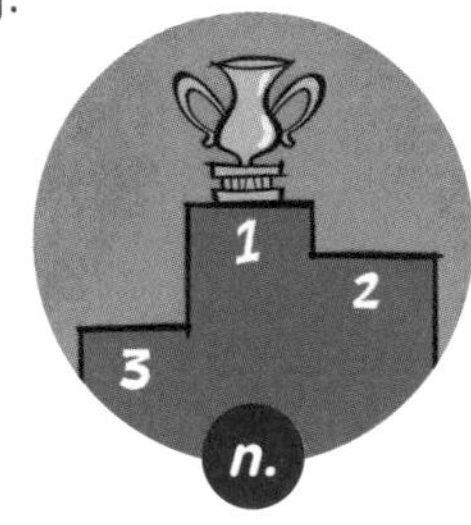

k.

l.

Verbs are doing or being words.

You add the suffixes **-ed** or **-ing** to the end of verbs to show tense. Tense tells us when something happens. Things can happen in the past, present or future.

These verb suffixes will help you in your writing all the time, so it's important to learn how to add **-ed** and **-ing** to different types of verbs.

REMEMBER!

Verbs ending in -ed talk about the past.

Verbs ending in -ing show that something is happening (right now) or was happening (in the past).

1

To most verbs, you simply add **-ed** or **-ing.**

walk

walk + ed → walked

walk + ing → walking

2

When a verb **ends in e**, you remove the final e before adding **-ed** or **-ing**.

love

lov~~e~~ + ed → loved

lov~~e~~ + ing → loving

3

When a verb **ends in a consonant and a y**, you have to change the -y to an -i before adding -**ed**.

try

try + i + ed → tried

4

When a verb **ends in a short vowel sound followed by a consonant**, you need to double the last letter first before adding -**ing** or -**ed**

short o vowel sound → ← p is a consonant

stop

stop + p + ed → stopped

stop + p + ing → stopping

Now, we are going to practise adding verb suffixes to words that end in **e**.

When a verb **ends in e**, you remove the final e before adding -**ed** or -**ing**.

love

love + ed → loved

love + ing → loving

REMEMBER!

-ed and -ing are verb suffixes. Verbs ending in -ed talk about the past. Verbs ending in -ing show that something is happening (right now) or was happening (in the past).

1 Circle the words ending in the suffix -ing that are spelled correctly.

a. dance → **dancing** / **danceing**

b. come → **comeing** / **coming**

c. give → **giving** / **giveing**

d. rise → **riseing** / **rising**

2 Transform these verbs into the past tense by adding -ed.

a. smile → ....

b. hope → ....

c. wash → ....

d. snore → ....

e. wave → ....

f. walk → ....

g. lick → ....

3 Complete these sentences.

Fill in the missing words using the options below and add **-ing**.

bake **hide** **write** **ride**

a. Plato is .... a blueberry pie.

b. Brick loves .... his bike after school.

c. Bogart is .... tips for taking over the world.

d. Armie is .... behind a bookshelf.

4 Complete these sentences.

Fill in the missing words using the options below and add **-ed**.

argue **please** **scare** **chase**

a. Yang .... Yin by dressing up as a ghost.

b. Oz was .... with her invention.

c. Bearnice .... after the ice cream truck.

d. Grit .... to stay up past his bedtime.

Next, we are going to practise adding verb suffixes to words that end in the letter **y**. However, there are two types of words that end in -**y**.

1 Words ending in a **vowel + y**

stay play buy

2 Words ending in a **consonant + y**

carry dry copy

When you want to add -**ed** or -**ing** to a word that ends with a **vowel + y**, you don't have to take off any letters.

stay

stay + ed → **stayed**

stay + ing → **staying**

1 Circle the words that end in a vowel + y.

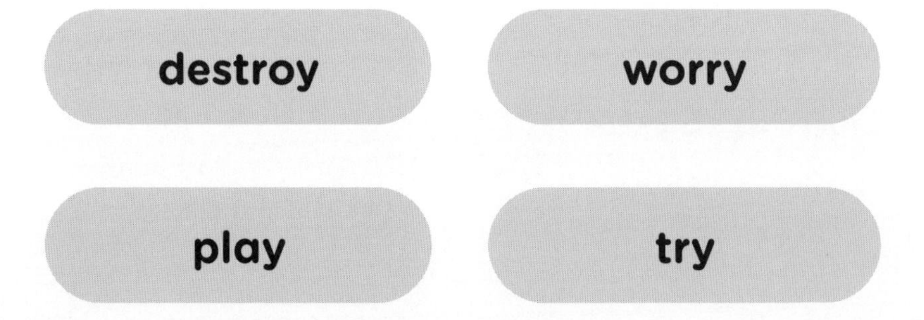

2 Add -ed and -ing to these verbs.

a. destroy → ....

b. play → ....

c. enjoy → ....

d. annoy → ....

When you want to add -**ing** to words that end with a **consonant + y**, you don't have to take off any letters.

try

try + ing → trying

However, adding -**ed** is a little different.
When you want to add -**ed** to words that end with a **consonant + y**, you first have to change the **y** to an **i**.

try

t~~ry~~ + i + ed → tried

3 Complete these sentences.

Choose the best verb and add -**ed**.

carry	**worry**	**dry**
spy	**fry**	**copy**

a. Plato .... potatoes for his dinner.

b. Brick .... Bearnice all the way home.

c. Bogart .... all of Plato's test answers.

d. The football pitch .... quickly after the rain.

e. Bearnice .... about the spelling test.

f. Yang .... on her sister to find out her secrets.

Finally, we are going to practise adding verb suffixes to words that end in a **short vowel sound** followed by a **consonant**.

When you add -**ing** or -**ed** to a word that has a **short vowel sound** followed by a **consonant**, you need to double the last letter first before adding -ing or -ed.

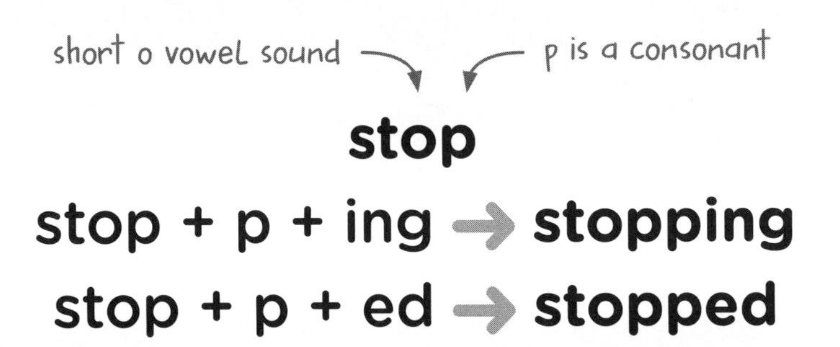

REMEMBER!

-ed and -ing are verb suffixes. Verbs ending in -ed talk about the past. Verbs ending -ing show that something is happening (right now) or was happening (in the past).

1 Circle the correct spelling.

Which words ending in -ed or -ing are spelled correctly?

a. hug → **huged** / **hugged**

b. jog → **joged** / **jogged**

c. nap → **napping** / **naping**

2 Complete these sentences.

Fill in the missing words using the options below.
Don't forget to double the last letter and add -**ed**.

beg **slip** **hop**

a. Brick .... over the fence like a ballet dancer.

b. "Please, please, PLEASE can I have the last cookie?"

.... Yang.

c. Grit .... on a banana peel and went flying into a bees' nest.

3 Complete these sentences.

Fill in the missing words using the options below.
Don't forget to double the last letter and add -**ing**.

swim **chop** **shop** **plan**

a. "I need a new hat. Let's go ....!" said Oz.

b. Bearnice loves .... in the sea.

c. Bogart was .... to take over the world.

d. Plato was .... onions for three hours.

You can add the suffixes -**er** and -**est** to some words.

Adding -**er** means "**more**".
Warm**er** means more warm.

Adding -**est** means "**most**".
Warm**est** means the most warm.

But not all words that take -**er** and -**est** add it in the same way.

For some words, you just add an -**er** or an -**est**:

old + er → older
old + est → oldest

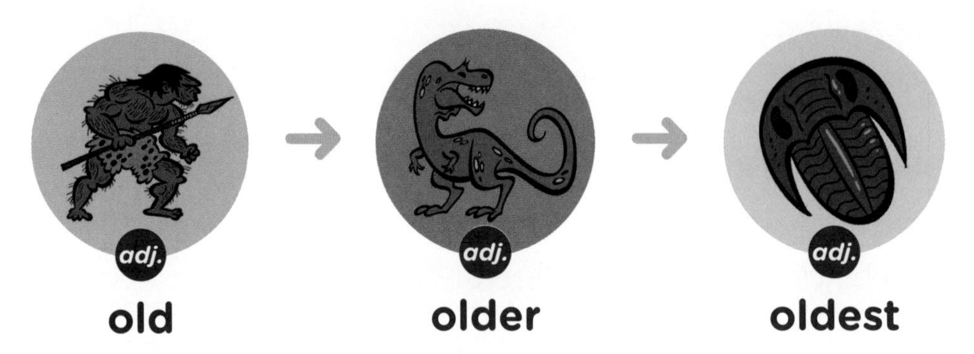

old **older** **oldest**

For words that **end in e**, you remove the final e before adding -**er** or -**est**:

nice + er → nicer
nice + est → nicest

nice **nicer** **nicest**

1 Fill in the missing words!

Use the pictures and the spelling rule to help you.

a.

close .... **closest**

b.

.... **higher** ....

c.

.... **fullest**

d.

fast ....

For words that end in **y**, you take off the **y** and add an **i** before adding -**er** or -**est**:

~~angry~~ + i + er → angrier

~~angry~~ + i + est → angriest

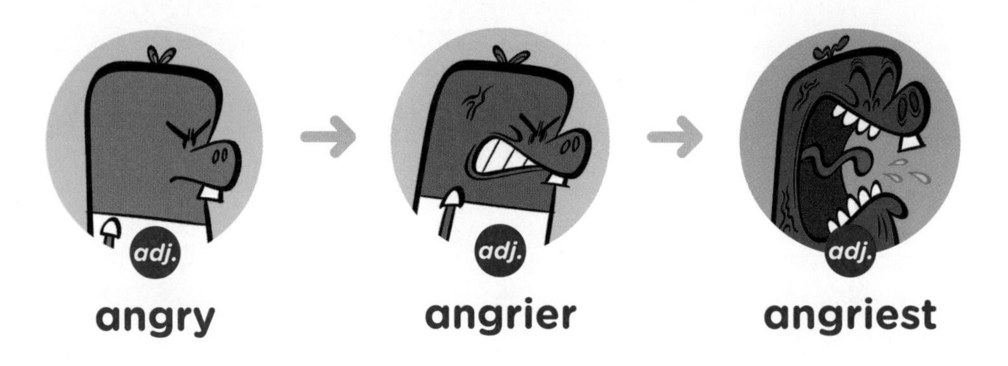

angry **angrier** **angriest**

For words with a **short vowel sound** followed by a **consonant**, you double the last letter and then add -**er** or -**est**:

hot + t + er → hotter

hot + t + est → hottest

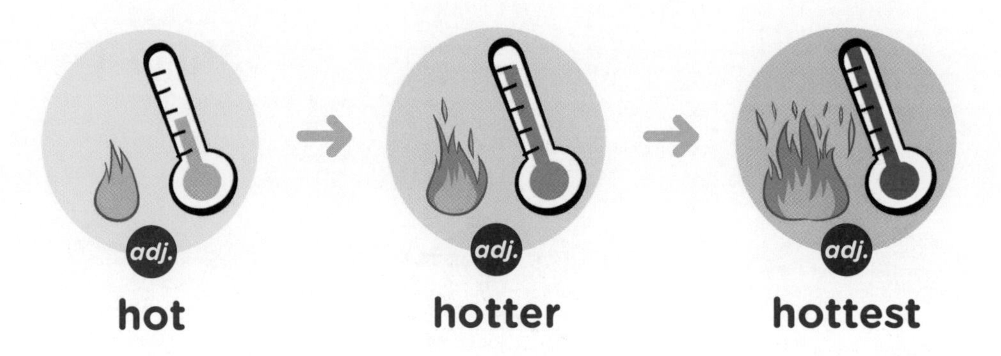

hot **hotter** **hottest**

2 Add -er suffixes and fill in the blanks.

Fill in the blanks with the words below. You will need to add or take away letters from some words before you can add the **-er**.

quick **warm** **close** **young**

a. Tomorrow, the weather will get a little bit ....

b. Oz wished she had a .... sister.

c. The .... you run, the sooner you'll get there!

d. Bearnice took one step .... to the giant cake.

3 Add -est suffixes and fill in the blanks.

Fill in the blanks with the words below. You will need to add or take away letters from some words before you can add the **-est**.

ripe **big** **hungry** **heavy**

a. Plato went straight for the .... slice of pizza.

b. Brick offered to carry the .... bag.

c. "This is the .... I've ever been!" roared Bearnice, rubbing her belly.

d. Oz only picked the .... apples off the tree.

You can turn some words into adjectives
by adding the letter **y** to the end of the word.

Not all of these adjectives add -**y** in the same way.
There are three different ways to do it.

For some words, you just add -**y**:

sand + y → sandy

For words with a **short vowel sound** followed by a **consonant**,
you double the last letter and add -**y**:

sun + n + y → sunny

For words that end in **e**, you take off the **e** and add -**y**:

cuddle + y → cuddly

1 Which spelling is right?

Cross out the wrong spelling in each sentence.
Use the rules above to help you.

a. This hot sauce is way too **spicy / spicey**!

b. It's very **noissy / noisy** in here.

c. My feet were all **sandy / sanddy** after walking on the beach.

d. The cheese on this pizza is so **stringey / stringy**!

e. The **greedey / greedy** goblin gobbled all the grapes.

f. I only wear **spoty / spotty** socks.

2 Can you help finish this weather forecast?

Turn these words into adjectives using the rules on the opposite page. Write an adjective that ends with **-y** under each image.

sun **wind** **haze**

rain **snow** **frost**

a.

Monday will be

....

b.

Tuesday will be

....

c.

Wednesday will be

....

d.

Thursday will be

....

e.

Friday will be

....

f.

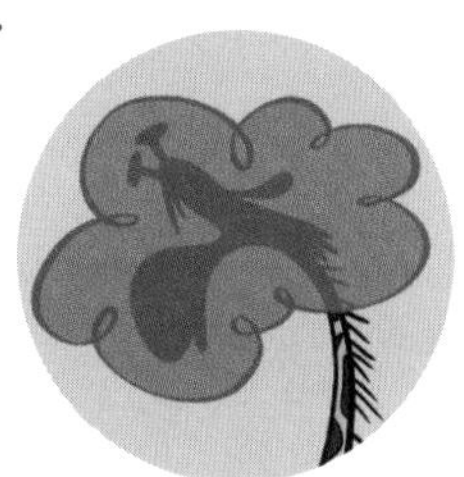

Saturday will be

....

You have already learned that adverbs describe verbs.
Remember, a verb is a doing or being word.
Adverbs describe how or when we do things.

EXAMPLES

You can turn some adjectives into **adverbs** by adding **-ly** to the end of them:

quick + ly → quickly

If the adjective ends in a **-y**, like **happy**, you first have to remove the **y** and add an **i** before adding **-ly**:

happy + i → happily

1 Rewrite these sentences using adverbs.

The words in bold describe the action of the verb. Turn them into adverbs using the rules above. The first one is done for you.

a. Yin answered the question **in an honest way**.

Yin answered the question honestly.

....

....

b. Plato laughed **in a loud way**.

....

c. Oz yawned **in a lazy way**.

....

d. Bogart ate the pizza **in a hungry way**.

e. Shang High closed the door **in a sad way**.

f. Brick waited **in a patient way**.

g. Bearnice looked around **in a nervous way**.

h. Armie poured his cereal **in a grumpy way**.

Some words are a little more tricky to spell than others. These words don't follow the rules we expect them to follow.

Some people call these exception words. We call them **rebel words**.

EXAMPLE

For example, from the way it's pronounced, you'd expect **busy** to be spelled "bizzy". But **busy** is too **busy** to follow the rules...

These are words we have to learn by heart, and it can be fun to practise them in different ways.

1 Copy out these rebel words.

Copy out each rebel word and read it aloud to hear which letters don't make the sound you would expect.

water .... water

clothes ....

child ....

eye ....

people ....

beautiful ....

parents ....

behind ....

2 Complete the sentences.

Choose the correct spelling and fill in the blanks.

a. Yin poked Yang in the ....

eye / **ai**

b. Bearnice hid her diary .... the sofa.

behind / **buhind**

c. Oz has .... for every occasion.

cloathes / **clothes**

d. Brick drinks lots of .... after weightlifting.

water / **wawter**

e. The sunset looked ....

butiful / **beautiful**

f. Armie's .... loved to read just as much as he did.

parents / **perents**

g. The .... had the best imagination.

child / **chiled**

h. The busy city centre was full of ....

people / **peeple**

READING AND WRITING

Here, you will read stories, poems and diaries, as well as pieces of writing that tell you something about the real world. You will answer some questions about each text and some questions that ask you to practise skills that you learned in the rest of the book. At the end of this section there are prompts to help you take your writing to the next level.

PLATO'S TRIP TO THE MARKET

In this section, we're going to focus on **reading comprehension** skills when reading fiction texts. Reading comprehension is all about reading a text carefully, taking your time, and understanding it. Reading longer texts helps you build up your reading stamina and fluency.

First, we're going to get into the mood for a story about food by learning some tasty new words.

Then, when you have read through these new words, turn the page and read the story about Plato's trip to the market.

Finally, use the text to help you answer the questions. If you aren't sure about an answer, go back and read the text again.

DID YOU KNOW?

Fiction texts are made up and come from the writer's imagination.

tasty taco

spicy chili

black pepper

creamy avocado

juicy tomato

crunchy carrots

fresh bread

cheesy pizza

wild mushrooms

steamed dumplings

tempting mangoes

red onions

smelly cheese

flaky fish

Plato was tired of making the same old taco fillings every day. He'd lost interest in creamy avocados. He'd had enough of flaky fish. He couldn't face seeing one more juicy tomato.

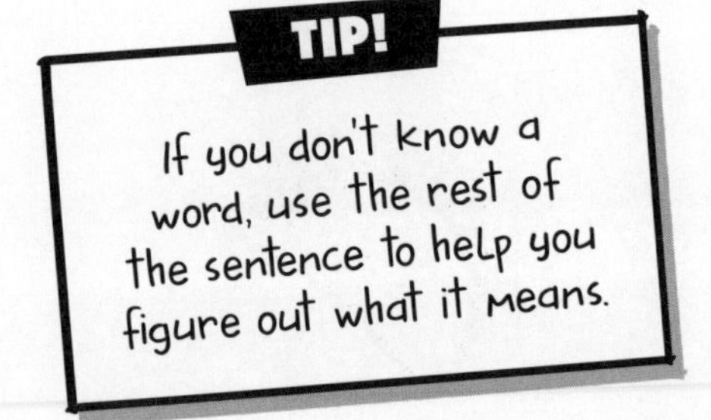

Sure, his tacos were flavourful. Everyone knew they were delicious. But were they spicy enough? Plato wanted to create a taco so spicy that his name would go down in history.

He needed new ideas. He needed new ingredients. He needed to go to the market!

The market was crowded when Plato arrived. It was full of colours and smells. He saw tables piled high with fruit, vegetables and buckets of herbs.

"Look at these tempting mangoes!" said one shopkeeper, as Plato walked by.

Plato searched everywhere for a life-changing ingredient. And then he saw something in the distance. It was the chilli stall.

First, Plato tasted a big, red chilli and it was spicy, but not spicy enough. Then, he tasted a medium-sized, red chilli and it was spicier, but it still wasn't spicy enough.

Finally, just as he was about to give up, Plato spotted a tiny, green chilli the size of a pea. He lifted it to his mouth, stuck out his tongue and licked it very carefully.

"Woah!" cried Plato. "My tongue feels like it's on fire!"

Plato knew he had found what he was looking for! He rushed home.

1 Who is the main character in this story?

....

2 Can you find a synonym of tasty?

The writer of the story uses adjectives to describe Plato's tacos. Can you find an adjective that means **tasty**? Write it here:

REMEMBER!

A synonym is a word that means the same or nearly the same as another word.

....

3 Check the correct answer.

How does Plato feel at the beginning of the story?

4 Why does Plato feel that way at the beginning?

....

....

5 What kind of tacos does Plato want to make?

....

6 What was for sale at the market?

Check all the items you can find in the text.

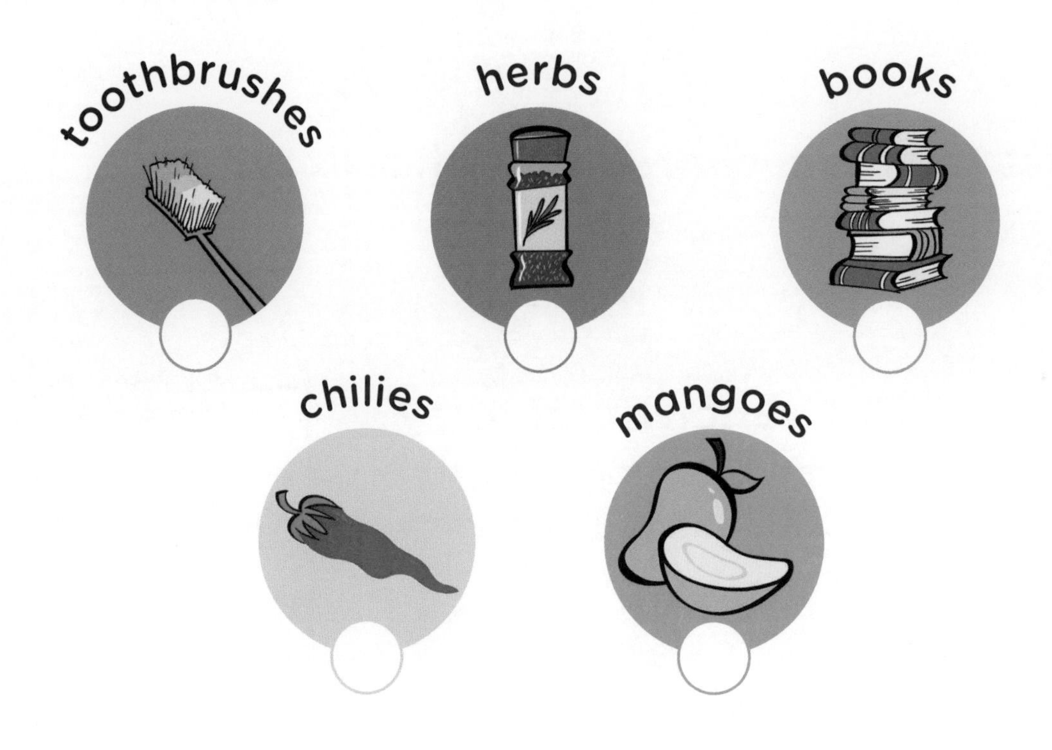

7 Circle the correct answer.

Why did the shopkeeper tell Plato to look at the tempting mangoes?

a. He wanted Plato to buy his mangoes.

b. He wanted Plato to steal his mangoes.

c. He was eating some mangoes.

8 Can you order these events?

In which order did these things happen in the text?
Write the numbers 1 to 4 in the boxes.

Plato tasted a green chili.

Plato saw some tempting mangoes.

Plato tasted a medium-sized, red chili.

Plato decided to go to the market.

9 Why do you think Plato's tongue feels like it's on fire?

....

....

10 What happens next?

What do you think will happen when Plato gets home?
Try to base your answer on what you already know from the text.

....

....

PLANET EARTH FACT FILE

In this section, we'll be reading two **non-fiction** texts about Planet Earth. Take your time as you read and use the texts to help you answer the questions that follow.

Some of the questions will test your understanding of the text. Some of the questions will ask you to practise skills that you learned in the rest of this book.

Let's start by learning some Earth words to get us in the zone!

TIP!

Non-fiction texts are based on facts and teach something to the reader.

tall mountain

tropical island

lush rainforest

long river

enormous iceberg

grassy meadow

green field

coral reef

shallow pond

cold glacier

rocky canyon

deep ocean

rolling hills

sandy beach

TEXT 1

The Pacific Ocean is the deepest ocean on our planet.

It has twice as much water in it as the Atlantic Ocean.

The driest place in the world is the Atacama Desert.

It is in South America.

Antarctica is the coldest place on Earth.

Some people call it the South Pole.

1 **Find and copy out one of the facts from the text.**

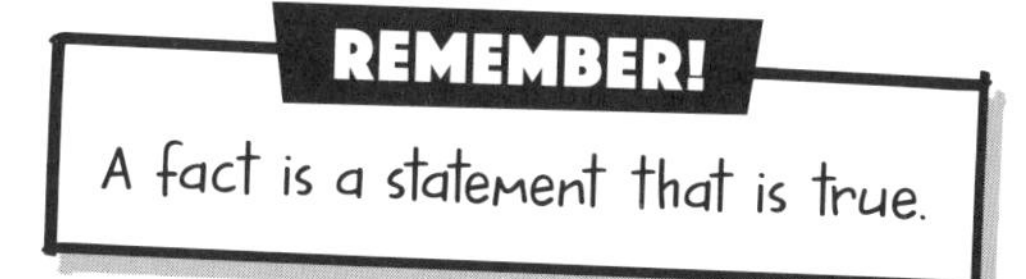

2 **Which of these words have opposite meanings?**
Circle the correct answer.

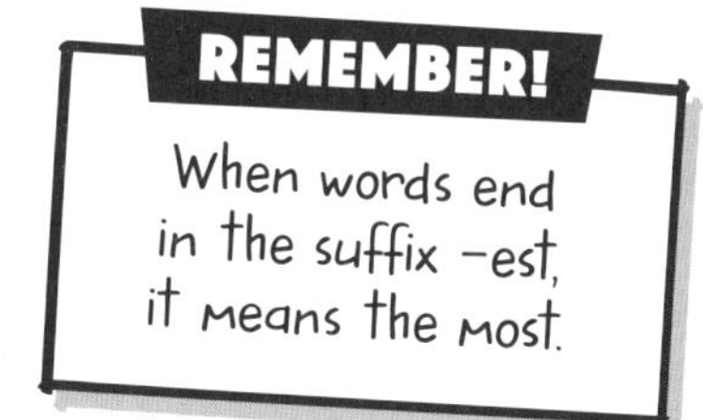

a. The opposite of **driest** is

smallest **hottest** **wettest**

b. The opposite of **deepest** is

largest **shallowest** **coldest**

c. The opposite of **coldest** is

hottest **darkest** **biggest**

3 **Which place is coldest?**
Check the correct answer.

4 **Is this true or false?**
"The Atlantic Ocean has less water than the Pacific Ocean."

TEXT 2

The biggest rainforest on Earth is called the Amazon.

It is so big that it spreads across nine different countries!

The Nile is the longest river on Earth.

It flows through Egypt all the way to the sea.

Mount Everest is the tallest mountain on the Earth's surface.

It is in a country called Nepal.

5 Write the name of the country.

a. Where should you go if you want to climb to the highest point on Earth?

....

b. Where will you find the longest river?

....

6 Put these words in order to make sentences.

Use the capital letters to help you.

a. mountain Nepal tallest The is in.

....

....

REMEMBER!

Capital letters go at the start of a sentence and at the start of place names, like Egypt.

b. river There long in Egypt is a.

....

c. share Amazon rainforest the countries Nine.

....

7 Now complete these facts about yourself!

a. The tallest person in my family is ....

b. The longest book I have read was called ....

....

ANIMAL POEMS

In this section, we'll be looking at **poems** about animals. Take your time as you read and use the poems to help you answer the questions that follow.

Some of the questions will test your understanding of the text. Some of the questions will ask you to practice skills that you learned in the rest of this book.

Before we read an animal poem, let's start by learning some words to describe wild animals!

booming

adj. very loud

WORD PAIRS

booming **voice**
booming **speakers**
booming **music**

bushy

adj. thick and fluffy

WORD PAIRS

bushy **tail**
bushy **eyebrows**
bushy **hair**

graceful

adj. moving in a smooth and controlled way

WORD PAIRS

graceful **dancer**
graceful **twirl**
graceful **leap**

knobby

adj. lumpy or uneven

WORD PAIRS

knobby **knees**
knobby **tree**
knobby **knuckles**

matted

adj. tangled or thickly knotted

WORD PAIRS

matted **hair**
matted **fur**
matted **wool**

1 Connect the words to the matching picture.

Can you draw a line from these pictures to the words that describe them?

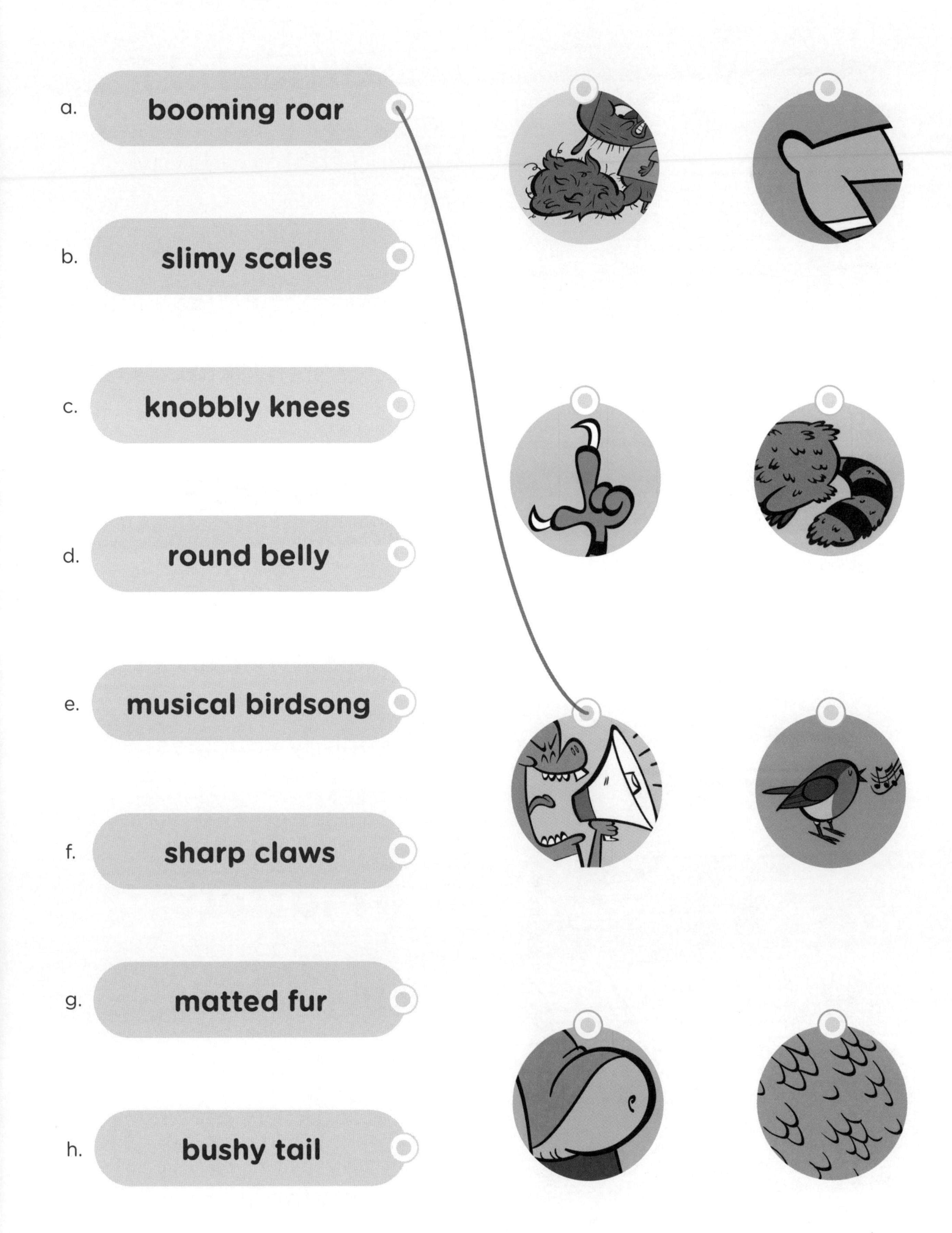

ARE YOU READY TO READ AN ANIMAL POEM?

Let's go over what we know about poems one more time.

Poems express a feeling, an idea or a story. An important thing to remember about poems is that they aren't always written in full sentences, but they are always written in **lines**.

The lines in a poem can be grouped together to make **verses**. In poems, verses work a bit like paragraphs.

Some poems **rhyme**. In poems that rhyme, the lines end with words that sound the same, like **walk** and **talk**.

Now turn the page to find our first poem!

Wild Wild Animal Rock

Here comes the hippo with the booming roar,
He's the singer in a band called Jungle Explore.

His friend, the bear, who bashes the drums,
Clutches drumsticks between her fingers and thumbs.

The graceful ostrich, a lively prancer,
Joined the band as a backup dancer.

Two twin tigers tinkle on the keyboard,
Sharp claws tapping, so they can't be ignored.

The DJ giraffe with knobbly knees,
Mixes songs so smoothly it feels like a breeze.

Their pal, the platypus, with matted fur,
Plays guitar so quickly that his fingers blur.

A shy armadillo hides just off stage,
Managing the band and staying out of the way.

These animals make a fantastic show.
If you get a chance to see them,
You really must go!

2 Circle the right answer.

How does the writer of this poem **feel** about the animal rock band?

She doesn't know them. | **She thinks they are very good.** | **She finds them boring.**

3 Which of the animals does not enjoy performing?

Find the answer in the poem.

....

4 Find the rhymes!

Can you find the words in the poem that rhyme with the words below?

a. **Thumbs** rhymes with ....

b. **Fur** rhymes with ....

c. **Go** rhymes with ....

5 Find the right shade of meaning.

Circle the phrase that best describes these words.

a. **Booming** means: **very quiet** | **loud** | **very loud**

b. **Fantastic** means: **very bad** | **good** | **very good**

6 Circle the instruments in the poem.

Which of these instruments does the writer mention?

keyboard | **violin** | **drums**

guitar | **trumpet**

NOW WE'RE GOING TO READ ANOTHER ANIMAL POEM.

This one is by **Lewis Carroll**.

Lewis Carroll wrote this poem over 150 years ago, in **1865**.
It was included in his novel, **Alice's Adventures in Wonderland**.

Lewis Carroll uses some archaic words in his poem.
Archaic means old, so don't worry if you don't understand what every word means!

How Doth the Little Crocodile

How doth the little crocodile
Improve his shining tail,
And pour the waters of the Nile
On every golden scale!
How cheerfully he seems to grin,
How neatly spreads his claws,
And welcomes little fishes in,
With gently smiling jaws!

Lewis Carroll

7 Underline the right answer.

What does the crocodile do to the little fishes?

TIP!

This is a question where you have to work out the answer using the clues you are given in the poem.

a. He eats them.

b. He spits at them.

c. He high-fives them.

8 Can you find the adverbs in the poem?

Adverbs **describe verbs**. Remember, a verb is a doing or being word. Adverbs describe **how** or **when** we do things. They often end in -**ly**.

a. How does the crocodile in the poem spread his claws?

....

....

b. How does the crocodile grin?

....

....

9 Why do you think the crocodile is smiling?

This is a question where you have to use the information in the poem to make a good guess.

....

....

....

....

10 Rhyme time!

Choose a word to complete these rhymes.

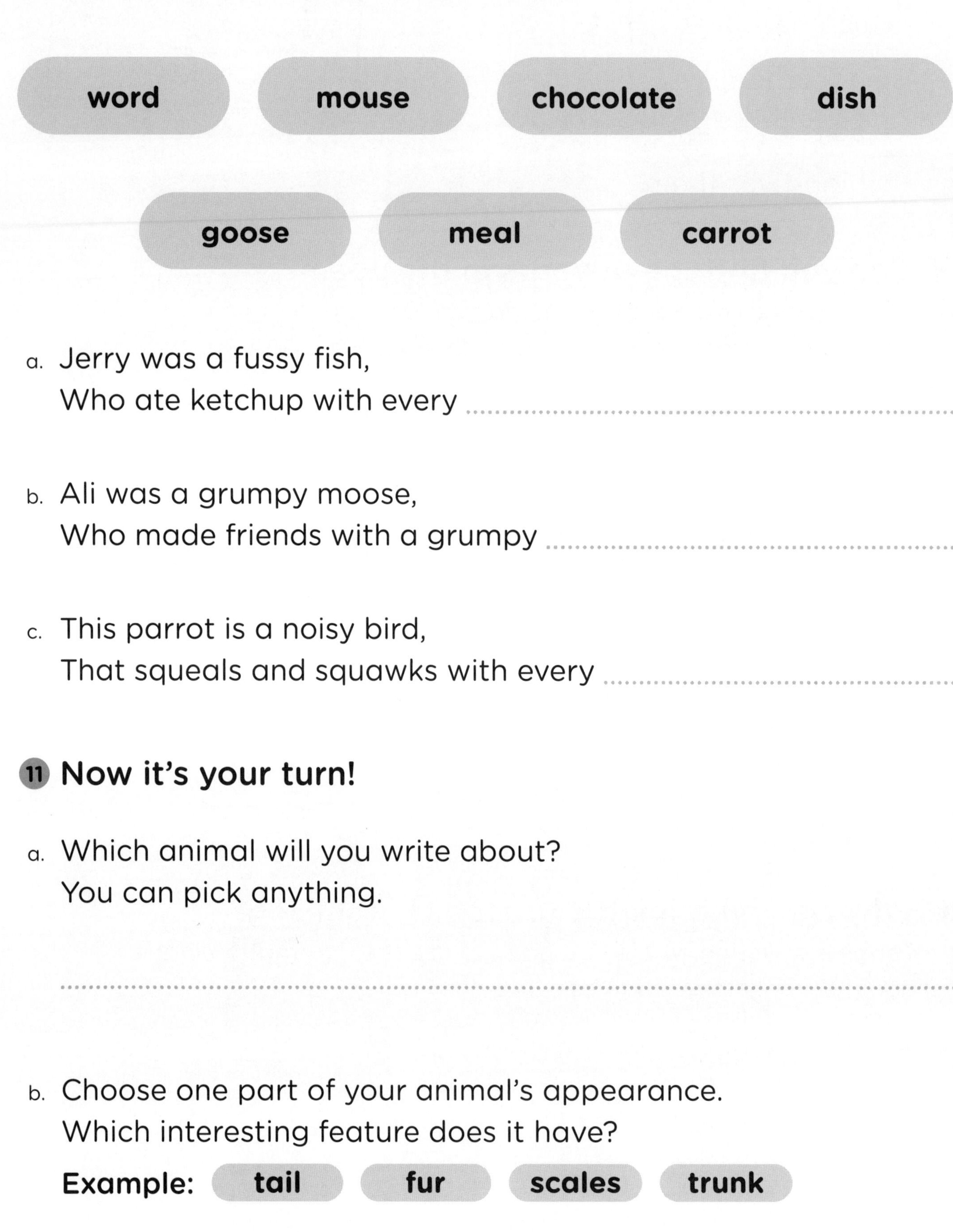

word mouse chocolate dish

goose meal carrot

a. Jerry was a fussy fish,
Who ate ketchup with every ....

b. Ali was a grumpy moose,
Who made friends with a grumpy ....

c. This parrot is a noisy bird,
That squeals and squawks with every ....

11 Now it's your turn!

a. Which animal will you write about?
You can pick anything.

....

b. Choose one part of your animal's appearance.
Which interesting feature does it have?

Example: tail fur scales trunk

....

c. Choose an adjective that describes this feature.

Example: **bushy** **slimy** **thick**

d. Now, try putting it all together to make an **expanded noun phrase**.

e. Finally, write two lines about your chosen animal!
For an extra challenge, see if you can make your lines rhyme!

GRIT'S DIARY

In this section, we'll be reading Grit's **diary**. Take your time as you read and use the texts to help you answer the questions that follow.

Some of the questions will test your understanding of the texts. Some of the questions will ask you to practise skills that you learned in the rest of this book.

DID YOU KNOW?

A diary is a place where you can write anything you want. It is a safe place to record all of your thoughts and feelings.

1 Three of these sentences come from somebody's diary.
Can you figure out which ones? Put a tick next to them.

a. Last night, I ate dessert before dinner!

b. The witch disappeared in a puff of smoke.

c. Then, we laughed all the way home.

d. I couldn't wait to tell my friends.

e. Do not press this button.

2 What do people write about in a diary?

What are some of the topics a person might write about in their diary? Write down as many as you can!

3 Grit needs some help!

He is writing his diary, but he needs help staying in the past tense. Can you help Grit choose the past tense form of each verb?

Part 1 - Saturday

Dear Diary,

Today, I had a bad day. It all started in the morning.

As I brushed my teeth, I (spill/spilled) spilled .... toothpaste everywhere. It got in my hair, it (cover/covered) .... the bathroom mirror and it (stain/stained) .... my brand-new t-shirt! That made me feel grumpy!

Then, my day got even worse when I rushed outside and (slip/slipped) .... on a slimy banana peel. I went flying across the street and (land/landed) .... on my bum!

Who left that there? I was so annoyed!

But that wasn't even the bad bit! A few minutes later, a bus drove through a puddle and (spray/sprayed) .... me with muddy water. I couldn't believe my luck! I was very angry!

By the time I got home, I was wet, cold and furious!

Yours,

Grit

4 Circle the statement that best describes Grit's day.

Grit felt better as the day went on.

Grit felt worse as the day went on.

5 Can you find the emotion words that Grit uses?

Grit uses different words to describe his emotions during the day. Circle the emotion words in the text.

Now write them here in the order that Grit feels them, as his grumpy feelings get stronger and stronger. The first one is done for you.

a. grumpy

b. ....

c. ....

d. ....

Part 2 - Sunday

Dear Diary,

This morning, I woke up with a big bruise from falling over, so I decided to cheer myself up and have sweets for breakfast. It was really hard to bite through the hard toffee, but so worth it!

After breakfast, I had a relaxing bubble bath to make myself feel better and listened to music. Then, I ate my favourite lunch of sausages with chopped-up sausages on top.

In the afternoon, I went to the park to say hello to the trees. Finally, when I got home, I rang Bearnice to tell her all about it.

Grit

6 What does Grit do to cheer himself up?

Circle all the correct answers.

go back to sleep	have a relaxing bath	write a letter
eat toffee	go to the dentist	scribble on the walls

7 Some words have more than one meaning.

Can you explain the two different meanings of **hard** in this sentence?

"It was really **hard** to bite through the **hard** toffee, but so worth it!"

....

....

....

....

....

8 Why do you think Grit rang Bearnice?

Underline the correct answer.

a. Bearnice is happy.

b. Bearnice ate all the toffee.

c. Bearnice is his friend.

TIP!

This is a question where you have to use the information in the text to make a good guess.

9 What is the correct order of events?

Looking at Part 1 and Part 2 of Grit's Diary, can you number these events in the order that they happened?

a. Grit got covered in water.

b. Grit talked to a friend.

c. Grit woke up feeling sore.

d. Grit spilled toothpaste.

e. Grit went to the park.

10 Now it's your turn!

Think of three things that you did yesterday. Now write them in the order that they happened!

REMEMBER!

You can use time adverbials to add information about when something happened, like "firstly", "next", "a little bit later" or "finally". Adverbials can go at the beginning or at the end of a sentence.

a. ....

....

....

b. ....

....

c. ....

....

11 Draw a picture of the best day you can remember!

What were you doing on that day? Why was it so good?
Make sure to include all the important details!

SUNFLOWERS

In this section, we will be reading a non-fiction text and a fiction text, and then comparing them. Both of the texts you will read are about sunflowers.

Take your time as you read and use the texts to help you answer the questions that follow.

Do you prefer reading fiction or non-fiction? Maybe this section will help you decide!

REMEMBER!

Non-fiction texts are based on facts and teach something to the reader. Fiction texts are made up and come from the writer's imagination.

TEXT 1 – How Sunflowers Grow

Sunflowers are tall plants with yellow petals. They are named "sunflowers" because they turn their heads to follow the sun from east to west every day. Sunflowers were first grown in North and South America, but now they grow all over the world.

All plants, including sunflowers, need six things to live: **water**, **light**, **suitable temperature**, **room to grow**, **air** and **time**.

When a sunflower seed has all of these things and is placed in soil, it will begin to grow. First, a little plant grows out of the soil. Then, it grows leaves. Over time, the plant gets much taller and grows a big, yellow flower.

1 Circle all the correct statements.

A plant needs water to grow.

A plant grows best in the fridge.

A plant needs WiFi to grow.

A plant needs light to grow.

2 True or False?

Circle the correct answer.

a. Sunflowers can grow all over the world.

true **false**

b. Sunflowers grow best in the dark.

true **false**

c. The flower is the first part of the plant to grow.

true **false**

3 Is this text fiction or non-fiction?

Remember, fiction is made up
and non-fiction is based on facts.

....

....

TEXT 2 - The Giant Sunflower

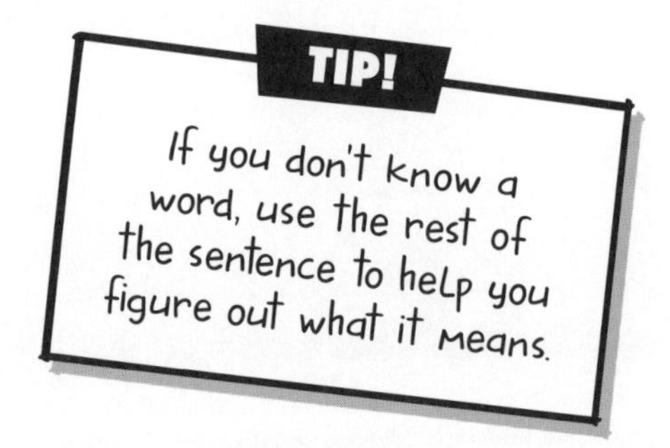

Armie loved gardening. He loved sharing his garden with the butterflies and the bees. Most of all, he loved his golden sunflower.

He planted his sunflower in the sunniest spot and he never forgot to water it. Every morning, he measured it proudly to see how much it had grown in the night.

One night, Armie woke up to a thundering crash coming from the garden. He looked out of his bedroom window and gasped. Something incredible had happened to his sunflower!

Armie ran down the stairs and out into the garden to get a closer look. His sunflower was enormous! The stem had grown so wide that he couldn't reach his arms around it. Armie was thrilled.

He looked up. The sunflower was the tallest thing he had ever seen. It went higher than the roof of his house. It went higher than the trees. It went up beyond the clouds. It was never-ending. Armie knew what he had to do. He started climbing.

4 Why do you think Armie planted his flower in the sun?

....

....

5 Why might somebody gasp?

Underline the correct answer.

a. because they are relaxed

b. because they are surprised

REMEMBER!

If you aren't sure about the answer, go back to the text to look for clues.

6 What type of noise is a thundering crash?

Circle the correct answer.

a loud noise

a quiet noise

7 Can you find a word in the story that is a synonym of big?

....

8 How did Armie feel when he first saw the giant sunflower?

Put a tick next to the correct answer.

upset

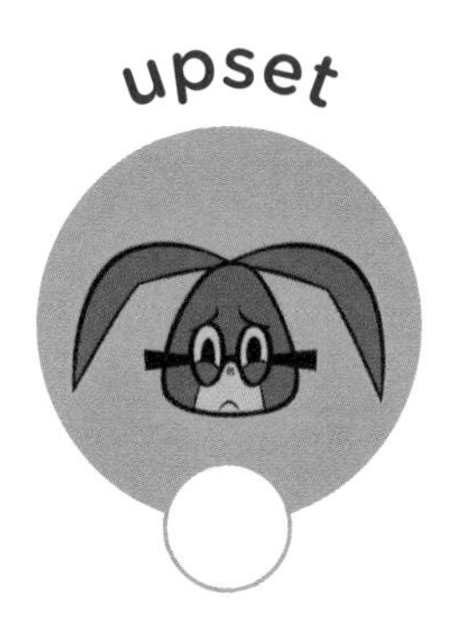

furious

happy

COMPARING THE TEXTS

How Sunflowers Grow (Text 1) and **The Giant Sunflower** (Text 2) explore the same subject in different ways.

Text 1 is non-fiction, which means it is based on facts and teaches something to the reader.

Text 2 is fiction, which means it is made up and came from the writer's imagination.

9 Can you find the facts that come from Text 1?

Put a tick next to each sentence that is a fact.

a. Sunflowers turn their heads to follow the sun from east to west every day. ○

b. Sunflowers have yellow petals. ○

c. Armie's sunflower grew taller than a house. ○

10 Can you find the sentences that are made up?

Text 2 is full of imaginative events that the writer made up. Put a tick next to the sentences that are made up (not facts) from Text 2.

a. Armie climbed a giant sunflower. ○

b. Sunflowers need water to grow. ○

c. Sunflowers were first grown in North and South America. ○

11 Which do you think is non-fiction?

Here are the titles of two different texts. Circle the title that you think is non-fiction.

Bearnice's Birthday Surprise

How to Make a Birthday Cake

12 Which do you think is fiction?

Here are the titles of two different texts. Circle the title that you think is fiction.

Where Elephants Live

The Talking Elephant

13 Can you think of titles for two new texts that are both about the **ocean**?

One is fiction and the other is non-fiction.

a. Fiction: ....

....

b. Non-fiction: ....

....

NOW IT'S TIME TO APPLY EVERYTHING YOU'VE LEARNED SO FAR AND GET WRITING!

In this section, you will need to write **at least three full sentences** based on a writing prompt.

Your first writing prompt is to write

about an astronaut landing on the moon and finding buried treasure.

GOALS

To help you get started, here are some goals for your writing:

1. Use at least two adjectives (words that describe nouns) to add descriptive detail.

2. Expand your ideas using the conjunctions **and**, **or** or **but**.

3. Use one exclamation mark for emphasis.

EXTRA CHALLENGE!

Try also using the conjunctions "because", "if", "when" or "that".

1 The first three sentences are written for you as a guide. Now, it's your turn!

Remember to base your writing on the prompt and try to use the goals to guide you!

adjectives

conjunctions

There was a **loud** thud **when** the **enormous** rocket landed on the moon. The astronaut stepped out **and** took a **deep** breath. What a **beautiful** view of the Earth there was**!**

an exclamation mark for emphasis

The astronaut looked left and saw

Your next prompt is to write at least three full sentences

about a fisherman who accidentally catches a mermaid.

GOALS

To help you get started, here are some goals for your writing:

Use two adjectives (words that describe nouns) to add descriptive detail.

Use one apostrophe in a contraction (to show where letters are missing in a shortened version of a word).

Use a synonym for happy or sad (synonyms are words that mean the same or nearly the same as another word).

EXTRA CHALLENGE!

Try using a word with the suffix -ful or -less in one of your sentences, like careful or careless.

3 The first three sentences are written for you as a guide. Now, it's your turn!

Remember to base your writing on the prompt and try to use the goals to guide you!

adjectives

It was a very **boring** day at sea. The **old** fisherman **hadn't** caught any fish all day. He was feeling **miserable** and **hopeless**.

contraction of had not

a synonym of sad

a word with the suffix -less

Suddenly, the fisherman saw something moving in the water and

HANDWRITING

In this section, you will learn about joining letters and get the chance to practise the most common handwriting joins. Being able to join your letters makes your writing faster and easier to read.

JOINING LETTERS

In this section, we are going to practise how to join letters. This skill can make your writing faster and clearer. Joins connect the ending of the first letter to the beginning of the second letter. We are going to practise four different joins.

Before you start, remember to:

Sit comfortably with your back straight and your feet on the floor.

2

Sharpen your pencil and hold it properly, with your fingers close to the sharpened point.

3

If you're writing with your right hand, tilt the page slightly to the left and if you're writing with your left hand, tilt the page slightly to the right.

1 Let's get practising!

Before learning how to best join different letters, let's warm up by first writing out all the letters of the alphabet.

a a b b c c d d

e e f f g g h h

i i j j k k l l

m m n n o o

p p q q r r s s

t t u u v v

w w x x

y y z z

The first join is a diagonal going from the baseline height of the first letter to the x-height of the second letter.

1 Practise the first join.

Follow the arrows to trace the letters in the example above.
Then practise writing the letters below, starting from the dot.

a. an an

b. am am

c. as as

d. ed ed

e. ew ew

f. in in

g. iy iy

2 Now, practise writing these words that contain the first join.

a. tin tin

b. air air

c. inn inn

d. hip hip

e. cup cup

f. kin kin

g. nip nip

h. any any

i. tiny tiny

The second join is a diagonal going from the baseline of the first letter to the x-height of the second letter and continues to the top of the ascender of the second letter.

1 Practise the second join.

Follow the arrows to trace the letters in the example above.
Then practise writing the letters below, starting from the dot.

a. it it

b. 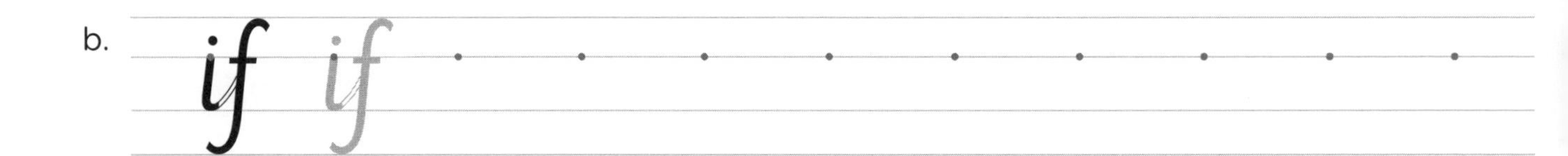
if if

c. 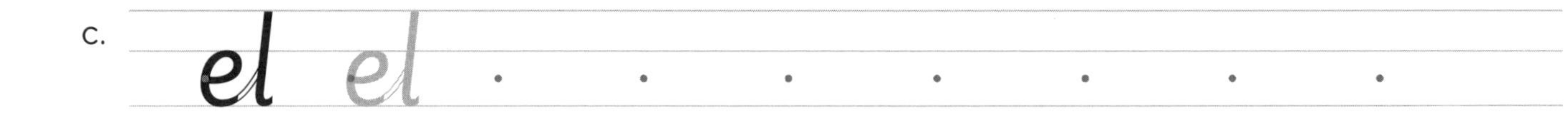
el el

d. 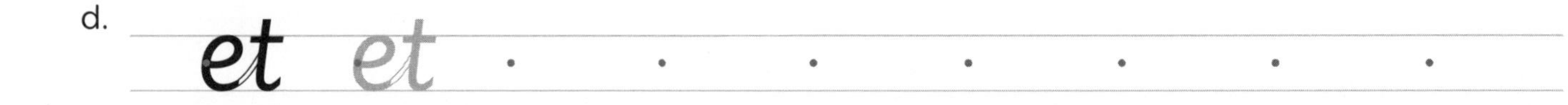
et et

e. 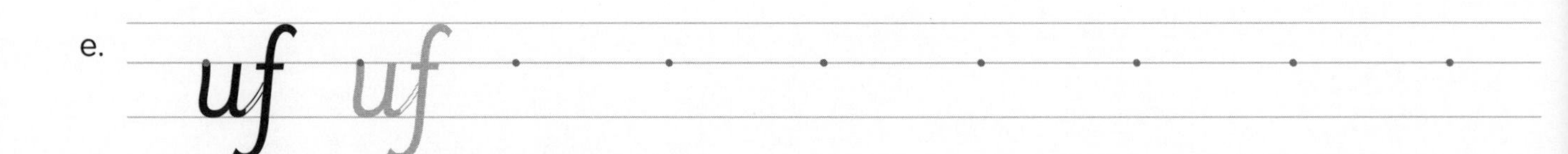
uf uf

f. ul ul

g. ch ch

2 **Now, practise writing these words that contain the first and second joins.**

a. *ink* *ink*

b. *all* *all*

c. *ant* *ant*

d. *cut* *cut*

e. *mint* *mint*

f. *mill* *mill*

g. *chill* *chill*

h. *think* *think*

i. *climb* *climb*

The third join is a horizontal line going from the x-height of the first letter to the x-height of the second letter.

1 Practise the third join.

Follow the arrows to trace the letters in the example above.
Then practise writing the letters below, starting from the dot.

a. on on

b. wi wi

c. rm rm

d. 

e. rv rv

f. fu fu

g. fy fy

2 **Now, practise writing these words that contain the first, second and third joins.**

a. land land

b. kind kind

c. lick lick

d. mind mind

e. luck luck

f. chuck chuck

g. talks talks

h. king king

i. thanks thanks

The fourth join is a diagonal going from the x-height of the first letter to the top of the ascender of the second letter.

1 Practise the fourth join.

Follow the arrows to trace the letters in the example above.
Then practise writing the letters below, starting from the dot.

a. ok ok

b. ot ot

c. ol ol

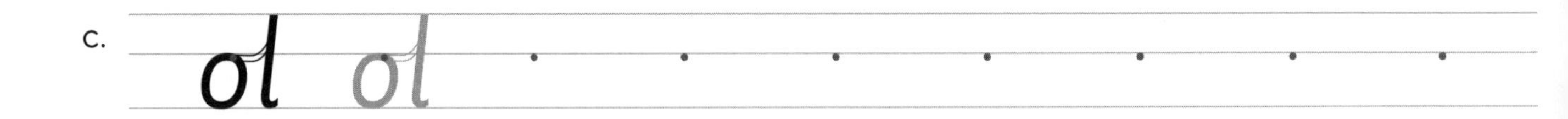

d. wl wl

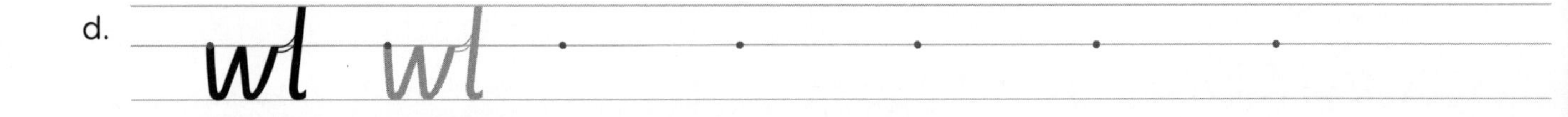

e. wh wh

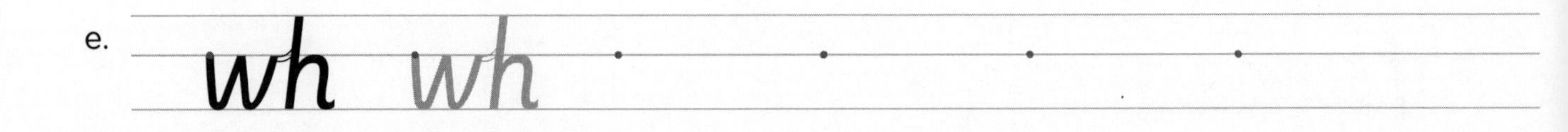

f. rb rb

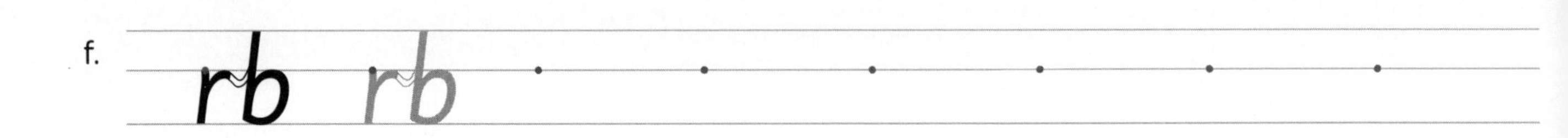

g. rh rh

2 Now, practise writing these words that contain all the joins.

a. our our

b. hour hour

c. worm worm

d. know know

e. harm harm

f. draw draw

g. find find

h. catch catch

i. leave leave

Pages 10-11

1 giggle, eat, catch, like

2 **a.** runs **b.** dances **c.** swims **d.** shines **e.** chases **f.** reads

3 **a.** laughing **b.** playing **c.** eating

4 **a.** drinking **b.** kicking **c.** baking

Pages 12-13

1 **Person or animal:**  **Plato**

Place:  **Earth**  **desert**

Thing:  **fruit**  **chair**

2 India, cheese, Oz, pencil, lizard (giggle, bite and run can also be nouns sometimes)

3 **a.** pizza **b.** Armie, library
c. frog **d.** Plato, Brazil
e. Yin, Yang, garden
f. Oz, marshmallows

Pages 14-15

1 **a.** huge **b.** evil **c.** slimy **d.** beautiful **e.** fried **f.** prickly **g.** unusual **h.** brave

2 **a.** hot **b.** tall **c.** spicy **d.** sticky **e.** fluffy **f.** red **g.** cosy **h.** howling

Pages 16-17

1 **a.** verb: laughed, adverb: happily
b. verb: moves, adverb: slowly
c. verb: ate, adverb: greedily
d. verb: sighed, adverb: sadly
e. verb: spoke, adverb: quietly
f. verb: rumbled, adverb: loudly

2 **a.** slowly **b.** messily **c.** tearfully **d.** joyfully

Pages 18-21

1 **a.** boxes **b.** hotdogs **c.** stars **d.** lunches **e.** paintbrushes **f.** sharks **g.** buses **h.** bananas **i.** torches **j.** peaches **k.** aliens **l.** paws

2 **a.** days **b.** boys **c.** keys **d.** trays **e.** toys

3 **a.** flies **b.** pennies **c.** cities **d.** fairies **e.** babies

4 **a.** foxes **b.** parties **c.** boxes **d.** toys **e.** books **f.** lorries **g.** beaches **h.** witches **i.** pies

Pages 22-23

1  **curly hair**  **blue sky**

 **soft fur**  **fizzy drink**

2 **Your answers might include:**
a. red **b.** sparkling **c.** kind **d.** deep **e.** dark **f.** elegant **g.** evergreen **h.** slippery **i.** hissing **j.** greasy

Pages 24-25

1 **a.** play **b.** watch **c.** cuddle

2 **a.** played **b.** pinched **c.** screamed

3 **a.** saw **b.** felt **c.** brought

Pages 26-29

1 b **2** c **3** c **4** c

5 **a.** E, S, Q, C **b.** Q, S, E, C
c. S, C, E, Q **d.** Q, E, S, C
e. S, Q, C, E **f.** S, C, Q, E

Pages 30-31

1 a wand, an orange, an egg, a tree

2 **a.** an **b.** a **c.** a **d.** an **e.** a

Pages 32-37

1 Brick grabbed his bicycle and cycled straight to the aquarium.

Grit didn't mean to be rude but he just wasn't in the mood for talking.

Oz was very tired but Bearnice's snoring kept her awake.

Shang High was usually listening to music or he was making music.

At three o'clock, Plato had a cup of tea and a piece of cake.

2 **a.** or **b.** but **c.** and
d. but **e.** and

3 I can't wait to have a birthday party when I turn seven!

I ate ten waffles for breakfast because I was starving.

I don't want to get soaked if it starts raining.

I didn't know that crocodiles can't stick their tongues out!

4 **a.** because
b. when or because
c. when or because
d. if or when
e. that
f. when or if

5 Your answers might include:
a. ...because I was so excited to go on holiday.
b. ...when I saw a spider sat on my pillow.
c. ...because my friend made the silliest face.
d. ...and scored the winning goal!

Pages 38-39

1 **a.** in the morning
b. in the blink of an eye
c. last night
d. as quick as lightning
e. All of a sudden

2 **a.** bit by bit **or** after a short while **or** in no time at all
b. bit by bit **or** after a short while **or** in no time at all
c. later today
d. bit by bit **or** after a short while **or** in no time at all

3 Any of the four options are correct.

Pages 42-43

1 **a.** **Y**in and **Y**ang love to braid **B**earnice's hair.
b. **E**very **T**uesday, **A**rmie writes in his diary for half an hour.
c. **T**omorrow, **P**lato and **I** will have a food fight.
d. **I**t's dinner time and **Y**in is very hungry.
e. **Y**esterday, **P**lato ran out of toilet paper!
f. **A**fter a long day at school, **O**z fell asleep on the swings.

2 **a.** He eats cake.
b. Ice is cold.
c. Trees are green.
d. I love December.

3 **a.** They walked home.
b. She swims on Fridays. (also correct: On Fridays, she swims.)

Pages 44-45

1 **a.** Bearnice went to the shop to buy apples, bananas, cookies, eggs and cheese.
b. Yang could play with Brick, Bogart or Armie.
c. Plato likes to swim in pools, lakes, streams and rivers.
d. Oz could sit on the bed, chair, toilet or sofa.

  e. Grit visited a farm with lots of chickens, pigs, cows, ducks and mice.
  f. Yin's pencil case contains pencils, pens and rulers.

2 Your answers could include any flavours with commas between all the items except the last two.

Pages 46-47

1 **a.** Yang's scarf
  b. Plato's tacos
  c. Bogart's ice cream
  d. Brick's family

2 **a.** Yin's teddy bear
  b. Grit's skateboard
  c. Brick's new trainers
  d. Bogart's telescope
  e. Armie's book
  f. Plato's frying pan

3 **a.** This is Grit's phone.
  b. This is Bogart's robot.
  c. This is Bearnice's hat.
  d. This is Armie's laptop.
  e. This is Plato's cake.
  f. This is Yin's ring.

Pages 48-49

1 **a.** I'm **b.** You're **c.** She's
  d. We're **e.** They're **f.** You'll
  g. Wasn't **h.** Didn't **i.** Don't

2 **a.** We're flying.
  b. I'm sorry.
  c. It wasn't me.
  d. You'll fix it!
  e. She's very tired.
  f. Don't hurt my teddy bear!

Pages 52-53

1 **a.** unhappy
  b. redo
  c. unzipped
  d. untidy
  e. replay

Pages 54-55

1 **a.** colourful
  b. fearless
  c. successful
  d. endless
  e. thoughtful

Pages 56-57

1 **a.** agreement
  b. kindness
  c. sadness
  d. entertainment
  e. darkness

Pages 58-61

1 **a.** blue + berries = blueberries
  b. cow + girl = cowgirl
  c. star + fish = starfish
  d. rain + bow = rainbow

2 **a.** butter **b.** paper **c.** jelly

3 **a.** **bedroom** **b.** **meatballs**
  c.  **rainforest** **d.**  **keyboard**
  e.  **pancakes** **f.**  **airport**
  g.  **sunflower** **h.**  **popcorn**
  i.  **armchair**

4 **a.** birthday
  b. snowman, moonlight
  c. football, cheeseburger, milkshake
  d. goldfish, dishwasher

5 seaside, sunshine, thunderstorm, sailboat, raindrops

Pages 62-65

1 **a.** happy **b.** annoyed **c.** worried

2 hot cold, forwards backwards, up down, dark light, day night, slow fast, before after, smile frown

3 **synonyms:** shut close, giggle laugh, look see, sad upset, draw doodle, hop jump, quick fast, thin narrow, talk speak, boring dull, tasty yummy

antonyms: near far, play work, wet dry, start finish, easy hard, smooth bumpy, love hate, soft hard, tall short, lost found

4 **a. synonym:** washed
antonym: dirty
b. synonym: yell
antonym: whisper
c. synonym: ill
antonym: healthy
d. synonym: nice
antonym: mean

Pages 66-67

1 **a.** Yang **b.** Bogart **c.** Grit
d. Bearnice **e.** Plato **f.** Bogart

Pages 68-73

1 **piece**  **peace**

 **break**  **brake**

 **write**  **right**

2 piece of cake, peace on Earth, piece of paper, puzzle piece, “I come in peace”, peace and quiet, home in one piece, feel at peace

3 tail, sail, plane, bear, flower, mail, two, bee

4 **a.** too **b.** sun **c.** here
d. plain **e.** be

Pages 74-75

1 **a.** left **b.** play **c.** sink **d.** watch

2 **a.** **b.** **c.** **d.**

e.  **f.** **g.** **h.**

Pages 78-79

1 **a.** sn**ai**l **b.** sn**a**k**e** **c.** pl**ay**

2 **ai:** t**ai**l, tr**ai**n, m**ai**l
ay: holid**ay**, Frid**ay**, s**ay**
a_e: pl**a**n**e**, l**a**k**e**, **a**p**e**

3 **a.** tail **b.** holiday **c.** lake
d. mail **e.** plane **f.** Friday

Pages 80-81

1 **a.** g**ee**se **b.** j**ea**ns **c.** comp**e**t**e**
d. hon**ey** **e.** sunn**y** **f.** p**ie**ce

2 **ee:** g**ee**se, coff**ee**
ea: j**ea**ns, t**ea**
e_e: del**e**t**e**, comp**e**t**e**
ie: p**ie**ce, th**ie**f
y: empt**y**, sunn**y**
ey: chimn**ey**, hon**ey**

3 **a.** geese **b.** tea **c.** delete
d. honey **e.** empty **f.** piece

Pages 82-83

1 **a.** kn**igh**t **b.** b**i**k**e** **c.** l**ie** **d.** dr**y**

2 **igh:** kn**igh**t, br**igh**t, f**igh**t
i_e: b**i**k**e**, pol**i**t**e**, k**i**t**e**
ie: cr**ie**d, l**ie**, t**ie**
y: wh**y**, dr**y**, fl**y**

3 **a.** tie **b.** fly **c.** polite **d.** fight

Pages 84-85

1 **a.** t**oa**st **b.** sn**ow** **c.** ph**o**n**e** **d.** d**oe**

2 **oa:** r**oa**d, g**oa**l, t**oa**st
ow: sl**ow**, wind**ow**, sn**ow**
o_e: j**o**k**e**, ph**o**n**e**, n**o**s**e**
oe: d**oe**, t**oe**, f**oe**

3 **a.** toast **b.** snow **c.** phone
d. road **e.** window **f.** goal

Pages 86-87

1 **a.** food **b.** group **c.** glue
d. stew **e.** flute

2 **oo:** food, roof
ou: soup, group
ue: statue, glue
ew: chew, stew
u_e: flute, tune

3 **a.** chew **b.** glue **c.** tune
d. food **e.** group **f.** roof

Pages 88-89

1 **short oo:** cookie, book, wood, foot, cook, look
long oo: pool, tooth, boot, goose, noodles, smoothie

2 **short ea:** feather, weather, breakfast, head, treasure, bread
long ea: bean, meat, beach, leaf, peach, peas

Pages 90-91

1 **a.** squash **b.** watch **c.** swan
d. wasp **e.** swamp **f.** wand

2 what, wasp, quality, wash, squat, swamp

3 **a.** wand **b.** lock **c.** quarrel
d. socks **e.** wants **f.** stop
g. swallowed, wants

Pages 92-93

1 **a.** month **b.** brother **c.** oven

2 **a.** honey **b.** rush **c.** monkey
d. nut **e.** money **f.** drum
g. shovel **h.** glove **i.** oven

3 **a.** jumped **b.** gloves **c.** Mondays
d. plum **e.** Nothing **f.** gum
g. shovel **h.** other

Pages 94-95

1 **a.** draw **b.** small **c.** warm

2 **a.** ball **b.** jaw **c.** walk
d. call **e.** claw **f.** straw

3 **a.** call **b.** talking
c. warm **d.** yawn

Pages 96-97

1 **a.** hurt **b.** circus **c.** hammer
d. world

2 **ur:** burp, curly
ir: thirsty, birthday
er: hammer, herd
or: worse, world

3 **a.** worse **b.** thirsty **c.** herd
d. curly **e.** burped **f.** birthday

Pages 98-99

1 **c:** coat, car, camel, candle
k: keyboard, fork, park, milk
ck: sick, duck, lick, rock

2 **a.** car **b.** milk **c.** camel
d. rock **e.** coat **f.** candle

3 **a.** milk **b.** rock **c.** keyboard
d. sick **e.** coat

Pages 100-101

1 **a.** spicy **b.** cereal **c.** circus
d. bouncy **e.** race **f.** space

2 **a.** face **b.** spider **c.** mice
d. snake **e.** voice

3 **a.** rice **b.** pencil **c.** sword
d. cinema **e.** spoon **f.** circle
g. lettuce **h.** sock

Pages 102-103

1 **g:** giant, gem, magic, giraffe
j: jam, jigsaw, jog, jail
ge: cage, stage, huge, page
dge: badge, sledge, hedge, bridge

2 **a.** badge **b.** jog **c.** jam **d.** jail

3 **a.** page **b.** cage **c.** giant
d. gem **e.** giraffe **f.** magic

4 **a.** sledge **b.** huge **c.** stage **d.** jigsaw

Pages 104-105

1 gnome, gnat, write, know, kneel

2 **a.** knight **b.** wrist **c.** wrapper
d. knife **e.** write **f.** wrong

3 **a.** knife **b.** nose **c.** wrote
d. nothing **e.** rabbit **f.** knight

Pages 106-107

1 pupil, freckle

2 **el:** tunn**el**, tow**el**, lev**el**
le: cast**le**, midd**le**, simp**le**
al: hospit**al**, anim**al**, sand**al**
il: foss**il**, nostr**il**, pup**il**

3 **a.** sandal **b.** castle **c.** tunnel
d. hospital **e.** pupil **f.** nostril
g. towel **h.** fossil

4 **a.** simple **b.** level **c.** middle
d. fossil **e.** animals

Pages 108-109

1 **a.** reflection **b.** celebration
c. injection **d.** station
e. meditation **f.** question
g. action **h.** education
i. emotion **j.** competition
k. invitation **l.** pollution

Pages 112-113

1 **a.** dancing **b.** coming
c. giving **d.** rising

2 **a.** smiled **b.** hoped **c.** washed
d. snored **e.** waved **f.** walked
g. licked

3 **a.** baking **b.** riding
c. writing **d.** hiding

4 **a.** scared **b.** pleased
c. chased **d.** argued

Pages 114-115

1 destroy, play

2 **a.** destroyed, destroying
b. played, playing
c. enjoyed, enjoying
d. annoyed, annoying

3 **a.** fried **b.** carried **c.** copied
d. dried **e.** worried **f.** spied

Pages 116-117

1 **a.** hugged **b.** jogged **c.** napping

2 **a.** hopped **b.** begged **c.** slipped

3 **a.** shopping **b.** swimming
c. planning **d.** chopping

Pages 118-121

1 **a.** close, closer, closest
b. high, higher, highest
c. full, fuller, fullest
d. fast, faster, fastest

2 **a.** warmer **b.** younger
c. quicker **d.** closer

3 **a.** biggest **b.** heaviest
c. hungriest **d.** ripest

Pages 122-123

1 **a.** spicy **b.** noisy **c.** sandy
d. stringy **e.** greedy **f.** spotty

2 **a.** snowy **b.** sunny **c.** rainy
d. windy **e.** frosty **f.** hazy

Pages 124-125

1 **a.** Yin answered the question honestly.
b. Plato laughed loudly.
c. Oz yawned lazily.
d. Bogart ate the pizza hungrily.
e. Shang High closed the door sadly.
f. Brick waited patiently.
g. Bearnice looked around nervously.
h. Armie poured his cereal grumpily.

Pages 126-127

1 water, clothes, child, eye, people, beautiful, parents, behind

2 **a.** eye **b.** behind **c.** clothes
d. water **e.** beautiful **f.** parents
g. child **h.** people

Pages 130-135

1 Plato

2 flavourful or delicious

3 bored

4 Your answer might be something like:

"Because he is tired of making the same tacos" or "Because his tacos aren't spicy enough"

5 Plato wants to make spicy tacos (your answer must include the word "spicy").

6 herbs, chillis, mangoes

7 **a.** He wanted Plato to buy his mangoes.

8 Plato tasted a green chilli. 4
Plato saw some tempting mangoes. 2.
Plato tasted a medium-sized, red chilli. 3
Plato decided to go to the market. 1

9 Your answer might be something like:

"The chilli is so spicy that it feels like it is burning his tongue."

10 Your answer might be something like:

"Plato uses the spicy chilli to cook some very spicy tacos."

"When Plato gets home, he works on a spicy taco recipe."

Pages 136-141

1 Any complete sentence from the text is correct.

2 **a.** wettest **b.** shallowest **c.** hottest

3 The South Pole

4 True

5 **a.** Nepal **b.** Egypt

6 **a.** The tallest mountain is in Nepal.
b. There is a long river in Egypt.
c. Nine countries share the Amazon rainforest.

7 **a.** Any statement that is true about yourself is correct.
b. The title of the longest book you have read is correct.

Pages 142-151

1 **a.** **b.** **c.** 
d.  **e.**  **f.** 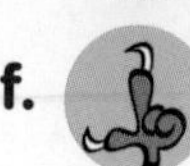
g. **h.**

2 She thinks they are very good.

3 The armadillo, or the shy armadillo

4 **a.** drums **b.** blur **c.** show

5 **a.** very loud **b.** very good

6 keyboards, drums, guitar

7 He eats them.

8 **a.** He spreads his claws **neatly**.
b. He grins **cheerfully**.

9 Your answer might be something like:

"The crocodile is smiling because he has tricked the fish and now he gets to eat them."

"He is smiling because the fish fell for his trick."

"He is smiling because he likes eating fish."

10 **a.** dish **b.** goose **c.** word

11 **a.** Any type of animal, like "a snake"
b. Your answer might be something like "scales"
c. Your answer might be something like "slimy"
d. Your answer might be something like "The slimy scales"
e. Your answer might be something like "The snake with the slimy **scales** had many adventurous **tales**."

Pages 152-159

1 a, c, d

2 Your answer might be something like "their day", "school", "a holiday", "a trip", "a dream" or "feelings"

3 spilled, covered, stained, slipped, landed, sprayed

4 Grit felt worse as the day went on.

5 **a.** grumpy **b.** annoyed
c. angry **d.** furious

6 eat toffee, have a relaxing bath

7 Your answer might be something like:

"Hard means difficult and hard also means not soft."

"Hard means difficult and hard also means difficult to bite."

8 c

9 **a.** 2 **b.** 5 **c.** 3 **d.** 1 **e.** 4

10 Your answer might be something like:

"I went to school."

"I played football."

"I listened to music."

"I saw my friend."

Pages 160-165

1 A plant needs water to grow.
A plant needs light to grow.

2 **a.** true **b.** false **c.** false

3 This text is non-fiction.

4 Your answer might be something like "He wanted his sunflower to grow."

5 b

6 a loud noise

7 enormous, wide, tall, high, neverending

8 happy

9 a, b

10 a

11 How to Make a Birthday Cake

12 The Talking Elephant

13 **a.** Your answer might be something like "The Mermaid's Ocean Adventure"
b. Your answer might be something like "A History of the Earth's Oceans"

CONCOCTED BY MRS WORDSMITH'S CREATIVE TEAM

Pedagogy Lead
Eleni Savva

Writers
Tatiana Barnes
Amelia Mehra

Academic Advisor
Emma Madden

Creative Director
Lady San Pedro

Designers
Holly Jones
Jess Macadam
Evelyn Wandernoth
James Webb

Lead Designer
James Sales

Producer
Leon Welters

Artists
Brett Coulson
Phil Mamuyac
Aghnia Mardiyah
Nicolò Mereu
Daniel J Permutt

With characters by
Craig Kellman

concoct
v. to make something by mixing ingredients

No animals were harmed in the making of these illustrations.

Project Managers
Senior Editor Helen Murray
Senior Designer Anna Formanek
Editor Nicole Reynolds

Senior Production Editor Jennifer Murray
Senior Production Controllers Louise Minihane and Mary Slater
Publishing Director Mark Searle

First published in Great Britain in 2022 by
Dorling Kindersley Limited
A Penguin Random House Company
DK, One Embassy Gardens, 8 Viaduct Gardens,
London, SW11 7BW

The authorised representative in the EEA is
Dorling Kindersley Verlag GmbH. Arnulfstr. 124,
80636 Munich, Germany.
10 9 8 7 6 5 4 3 2
002-326342-Mar/2022

A CIP catalogue record for this book
is available from the British Library.
ISBN 978-0-24153-205-8

Printed and bound in Malaysia

www.dk.com

mrswordsmith.com

For the curious

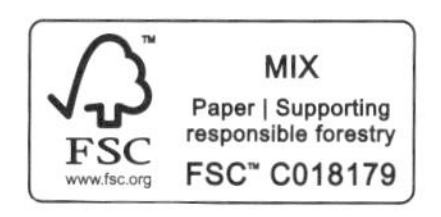

This book was made with Forest Stewardship Council™ certified paper - one small step in DK's commitment to a sustainable future.

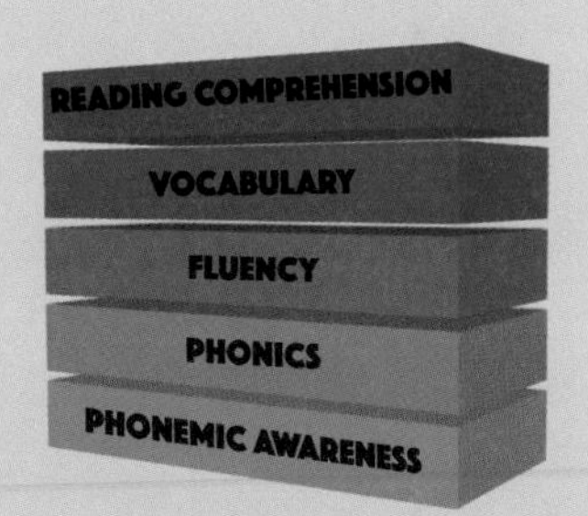

The building blocks of reading

READ TO LEARN

LEARN TO READ

Phonemic Awareness → Phonics → Fluency → Vocabulary → Reading Comprehension

Readiculous App
App Store & Google Play

Word Tag App
App Store & Google Play

OUR JOB IS TO INCREASE YOUR CHILD'S READING AGE

This book adheres to the science of reading. Our research-backed learning helps children progress through phonemic awareness, phonics, fluency, vocabulary and reading comprehension.